How Should
I Live?

ALSO BY RANDOLPH FEEZELL

FAITH, FREEDOM, AND VALUE:
Introductory Philosophical Dialogues 1989

How Should I Live?

Philosophical Conversations about Moral Life

Randolph M. Feezell

CREIGHTON UNIVERSITY

Curtis L. Hancock

ROCKHURST COLLEGE

PARAGON HOUSE
New York

First edition, 1991
Published in the United States by

Paragon House
90 Fifth Avenue
New York, NY 10011

Book Design by Deirdre C. Amthor

Library of Congress Cataloging-in-Publication Data
Feezell, Randolph M., 1950–
How should I live?: philosophical conversations about moral life/
Randolph M. Feezell and Curtis L. Hancock.—1st ed.
p.   cm.
Includes bibliographical references.
ISBN 1-55778-284-9: $14.95
1. Ethics.   I. Hancock, Curtis L., 1950–   .   II. Title.
BJ1025.F26   1991
170—dc20   90-20574
                                                  CIP

Manufactured in the United States of America

10   9   8   7   6   5   4   3   2   1

Contents

PREFACE 1

INTRODUCTION: To the Student 5

Dialogue One: What Is Ethics? 13

Dialogue Two: Ethics and Religion 39

Dialogue Three: Ethics and Relativism 59

Dialogue Four: Ethics and Self-Interest 85

Dialogue Five: Ethics and Consequences 107

Dialogue Six: Ethics and Persons 135

Dialogue Seven: Ethics and Virtue 170

Dialogue Eight: Ethics and Female Voices 190

EPILOGUE: Is Ethics Worthwhile? 210

Preface

In this book we have tried, like many ethics teachers before us, to provide an introduction to ethics. In most respects, our book is traditional. But we have decided to present the traditional and basic issues of ethics in a relatively nontraditional way. We have written a series of dialogues, philosophical conversations in which the participants engage in disputes about the basic principles and foundations of our moral lives.

FORM

We have presented the issues in dialogue form primarily for pedagogical reasons. Combined, we have taught ethics for over twenty-five years. We have become familiar with what students say and ask, course after course, semester after semester, year after year. The dialogue form offers a way to respond to student views in a more realistic and compelling manner than usual textbook presentations. We want to examine the issues in a way that is as clear, lively, and interesting as possible for students who will come to this book with little or no background in philosophy. Above all, we want the students to gain a sense of both the content of ethics and the process of philosophizing.

Philosophy isn't merely solitary reflection or scholarly devotion to the interpretation of significant historical texts. Philosophy isn't merely the possession of certain ideas or values, or the convictions that unify our different lives. Philosophy is active reflection, or, as Aristotle put it, a *habitus* of the intellect. It is, in an important sense, an activity of engagement, a pursuit, an inquiry that involves others who question, criticize, and challenge. The model, as always, is Plato's works, especially the early Socratic dialogues. In these dialogues, philosophy is brought into relation with the concrete concerns of life. For Socrates, philosophy wasn't idle chatter or abstract reflection. For him, philosophy was essentially related to questions about how we ought to live and what we ought to pursue. Our dialogues surely fall short of the literary and philosophical richness of Plato's; however, they are animated by commitments we share with him and others. We think philosophy is worthwhile, and we believe philosophical conversation is a great good. We also believe that the presentation of ideas in dialogue form can be uniquely instructive.

CONTENT

As we have indicated, many of the traditional issues of ethics are discussed in these dialogues. In the first dialogue, we attempt to give the student a sense of what ethics is about, and we raise questions concerning the extent to which ethics, or ethical reflection, is personal (or in some sense "subjective"), and impersonal, (or in some sense "objective"). In the second dialogue, we criticize the position that ethics is necessarily related to religion, or must be grounded in religious commitments. We criticize the so-called Divine Command Theory of morality, and we argue that ethical thinking is autonomous. The third dialogue offers fairly standard criticisms of both descriptive and normative relativism.

In the fourth, fifth, and sixth dialogues, we discuss, respectively, ethical egoism, utilitarianism, and Kant's basic deontological perspective. We attempt to be fair in offering the central ideas of each theory and in examining why some people have thought each to be an inadequate or incomplete account of our moral lives. Here the reader may sense a gentle progression from less to more adequate theories, or at least a developing understanding of the "thickness" of our moral lives and what an adequate theory would have to account for if it claimed to be a complete or thorough picture of morality.

The seventh and eighth dialogues are somewhat more unconventional for an introductory ethics book. The seventh dialogue attempts to present a clear picture of the centrality of virtue in our moral lives. Many introductory ethics texts simply ignore the so-called "ethics of virtue." This is regrettable, since such an omission neglects the entire natural law tradition, which dominated so much moral discourse in ancient and medieval times. Including a treatment of this important tradition makes our book distinctive.

The eighth dialogue is somewhat idiosyncratic for an introductory ethics book, but we think the topic deserves treatment. It is inspired by Carol Gilligan's work on moral development, and it discusses her notion that females typically approach and reconstruct moral situations according to an "ethic of care," as opposed to a "justice perspective" more typical of males. One can also interpret an ethic of care as a virtue ethic.

Finally, the epilogue furnishes a brief discussion of the value of ethics. This is an important topic since there is both uncertainty and disagreement, even among professional philosophers, about the nature and value of ethics as a discipline. There is even skepticism about the value of ethics courses.

We believe that each dialogue can stand alone, but we also hope that philosophy teachers will assign the chapters in order so the students will get to know each character and have a sense of progression in the dialogues.

PEDAGOGY

The quotations at the end of each chapter are meant to be clear expressions of the position critically discussed in the dialogue. The quotations are not meant to represent both sides of the debate. The criticisms of each position emerge as the dialogue progresses.

The questions at the end of each dialogue can be used for discussion. The student should read the questions carefully in order to focus on some of the main issues addressed in each dialogue and to guide further reflection on related issues. The teacher might also assign one of the suggested readings mentioned at the end of each dialogue.

The examples in the introductory chapter, "To the Student," can be used to generate initial discussion and to help students gain a keener sense of their own presuppositions when they begin to think philosophically about the issues discussed in the dialogues. The questionnaire also serves to make explicit these assumptions.

We believe our text is both highly accessible and challenging, appropriate for use on a variety of levels of course work. We hope that teachers and students will find this to be an approachable and useful introduction to ethics. It could be used along with primary sources, or as a main text, or as a treatment of ethical theory in the first part of a course on applied ethics. We also believe it is clear and nontechnical enough to be assigned as recommended supplemental reading in many ethics courses.

ACKNOWLEDGMENTS

We want to thank the Center for Health Policy and Ethics and the Graduate School at Creighton University for supporting this project. Various people at Creighton provided stimulating conversation that was helpful in clarifying parts of the manuscript; among them, Charles Dougherty, Joseph Allegretti, and Beverly Kracher. We also want to thank Nanci Borg and Peggy Troy for their tireless efforts in producing the physical manuscript. We want to acknowledge two members of the Rockhurst College community for their help toward the completion of this project. Both Dr. Thomas J. Trebon, dean of Arts and Sciences, and Wilfred L. LaCroix, S. J., chairperson of the Department of Philosophy, provided released time and some financial support. Additionally, the reviewers of this book made suggestions that have improved its quality and readability. We are grateful for the encouragement and editorial insights we received from the people at Paragon House, including Don Fehr, Jo Glorie, and Peter Coveney.

Finally, a word of thanks to Sandra Waddell, who understands, and to Alan Lacer, who for years was with us in the trenches, teaching ethics to bureaucrats.

Introduction:
To the Student

This book contains a series of philosophical conversations about the foundations of our moral life. We are often faced with moral decisions. Most of us have been taught the importance of at least some moral values, and many of us live as if such values are extremely important in deciding what to do, what sorts of things we ought to pursue, and what kind of person we should attempt to be. But when we begin to reflect on the moral dimensions of human life, we are faced with many puzzling questions. What is morality? Why do we have morality? Does morality have an object or purpose? Is there something distinctive about moral values as opposed to other kinds of values? Where do such values come from? Is there one basic principle at the root of our moral life? Are there a series of fundamental principles? What is it to be moral? How is morality related to self-interest? Why should we be moral? Or, why should we attempt to live a morally good life? Are moral principles subjective? Objective? Absolute? Relative? Can moral principles be rationally justified? Is morality basically a matter of feeling? Can we ever really know what is morally right or wrong? Are there any moral authorities? Are there moral experts? And so on!

Many of you have probably thought about some of these questions, and many of you may have some relatively strong opinions about them. On the other hand, many of you may be unsure about some or many of these questions. At least one value of taking an ethics course or reading a book concerned with philosophical ethics is that such activities provide the opportunity to engage in serious and sustained reflection on these important questions.

Following you will find a series of examples in which people have to decide what to do in certain situations. In some examples, people have made judgments about certain courses of action. The examples seem to have something to do with morality. Read through the examples. Attempt to decide what ought to be done. Ask yourself whether the example describes a "moral" situation or an instance of "moral" evaluation. Finally, after reflecting on the examples, answer the brief questionnaire. Be prepared to discuss your reactions to the examples and your responses to the questions.

1. Henry teaches philosophy at a university whose campus is physically unattractive. One of the features of the physical environment he finds most irritating is the condition of the university lawns. Students, faculty, and staff insist on walking on the grass, producing unsightly dirt paths. Such behavior appears to be caused by the desire of people to reach their destination (e.g., going to the library) a few seconds sooner. Henry finds such actions insensitive and usually attempts to persuade his students that the small convenience of taking a shorter route does not outweigh the value of more beautiful lawns. He believes people ought not to contribute to the gouging of university lawns.

2. Sophia is a Unitarian minister who has become deeply interested in the environmental movement. She has studied the work of Albert Schweitzer, who holds that the only acceptable ethic must have but one fundamental principle: Our actions ought to express a reverence for all life. She believes we ought to avoid injuring or harming anything that lives because we should hold all life sacred. She believes this ethical viewpoint has extreme implications, but she is now prepared to act consistently with the principle of reverence for life. She believes that we should become sensitive to the ethical significance of killing animals, smashing insects, even pulling weeds or cutting down trees for no good reason.

3. Harriet is having problems with her teenage son, a ranked tennis player whose behavior seems to be getting worse in the tournaments in which he plays. He seems to have copied the behavior of certain professional tennis players who scream, question calls, abuse officials, and never give any credit to the opponent. She thinks such behavior is wrong and that tennis is

causing her son to develop what she considers to be one of the greatest flaws in character: lack of humility. She is thinking about insisting that he either change his behavior or give up tennis. In her mind, having a good character is more important than being a successful tennis player.

4. Brad is a college student who is to graduate in May if he passes all his spring semester courses. He has waited until the last semester to fulfill his philosophy requirement because he has neither interest nor talent in philosophy. His final paper, which he has not written and is unprepared to write, is due tomorrow, and he will not pass the course unless he hands in the assignment. His roommate, Joe, who has taken the course under another instructor, offers to let Brad use his old paper to fulfill the requirement. There's a very high probability that Brad's instructor would never find out that he handed in a plagiarized paper. What should Brad do?

5. Pam is a college basketball player whose university has developed a random drug-testing program for athletes. Her father, a civil liberties lawyer and former athlete, has encouraged her to file suit against the athletic department to prohibit it from enacting the program. She also thinks it is wrong to invade the privacy of athletes and to single them out, but her coach has said that she would never be allowed to play if she files suit. She deeply wants to play. What should Pam do?

6. Nelson, a businessman, decides that he needs more traffic in his furniture store. He is considering an arrangement with a telemarketing company, in which people will be called and told that they have been chosen to receive a free gift from his furniture company, either a VCR or a gift certificate. The recipient must pick up the gift in person at the store. Of course, all of the recipients will receive the gift certificate, which is actually a coupon for a small reduction in price, if the customer decides to purchase some item. Nelson is certain that the plan will increase traffic in the store and help business, but he feels some slight problems of conscience, since he is not sure that it would be right to bring people into his store under such circumstances. What should he do?

7. Raymond, a lawyer, has been offered an excellent position as legal counsel for a very large and successful business whose primary product is fur coats. Raymond's fiancée, Barbara, is the president of a local animal rights organization. Barbara has convinced him that animals should be given at least *some* moral consideration, and that one of the most trivial and cruel ways in which humans use animals is for affluent people to wear fur coats. Barbara finds out that Raymond has been offered the job and insists that as a matter of principle he should turn down the job. What should he do?

8. Joan, a married woman, is traveling, doing business. She becomes acquainted with a man and finds herself physically attracted to him. He suggests that they go to his room. She realizes that her husband would never find out about her unfaithfulness, and she would very much like the pleasure of going to bed with this man. What should she do?

9. Mary, a young single mother of four, is on public assistance and is dependent on drugs. A sleazy acquaintance offers her a large sum of money if she would allow him to use her oldest daughter, who is thirteen years old, in a series of pornographic films. Mary desperately needs the money for her family, and she realizes that her daughter would participate in the pornographic films if she demanded it. What should Mary do?

10. Nick lives in Moronia, a country having a black majority population and a system of laws that systematically discriminates against blacks on the basis of race alone. Nick is the police chief of a small city experiencing increased racial conflict. He decides that he must act to dispel the unrest. He arrests the local black leadership, jails them without charges (which is legally allowed), and realizes that public statements by the leaders would calm the situation. He can get signed statements only by torturing the leaders, and then he intends to keep them in jail indefinitely. He would violate no laws by doing these things. What should he do?

ETHICS QUESTIONNAIRE

Write "A" for agree, "D" for disagree, and "U" for unsure.

____ 1. No one really knows what is morally right or morally wrong.

____ 2. We should deny that anyone can justifiably claim to know what is morally right or morally wrong because, after all, "who's to say what is right or wrong?"

____ 3. Morality is a matter of personal taste since it involves saying how an individual should act and individual values differ.

____ 4. What is morally right for me is not morally right for other people.

____ 5. It is very difficult to know the morally right thing to do, but sometimes, at least, we do.

____ 6. Morality is more a matter of "going with" your strongest feelings rather than "going with" what your reason tells you to do.

____ 7. Morality is an ideal system that is good in theory but not realistic in practice.

____ 8. Morality essentially involves considering the interests of others as well as my own interests when I act.

____ 9. A moral judgment is universal since it applies to everyone in similar circumstances.

____ 10. It is never morally appropriate to inflict suffering on a being without good reason.

____ 11. Moral claims are matters of opinion, not knowledge, since people disagree about what is morally right or good.

____ 12. All moral opinions are equal in validity since everyone has a right to his or her own opinion.

____ 13. Whatever is morally right is simply what I believe to be morally right.

____ 14. Some moral judgments are universally and objectively valid.

____ 15. Morality is simply a function of what the majority of people living in a particular society approve or disapprove of.

____ 16. Slavery is morally wrong wherever and whenever it occurs.

CAST OF MAIN CHARACTERS
IN THE DIALOGUES

PETER: A philosophy professor. He is English and speaks somewhat formally, perhaps because of his academic background and his English upbringing.

SOPHIA: A Unitarian minister. She is tough-minded, skeptical, outgoing, somewhat combative, and interested in environmental issues and feminism.

ROSE: Sophia's longtime friend. Sophia and Rose have known each other since high school. She is a mother of four, not particularly philosophical, and a good person.

RANSOM: The male guide of the backpacking expedition. He is working on a master's degree in Recreation Studies at a university and is a religious fundamentalist.

SARAH: The female guide of the backpacking expedition. She is working on a master's degree in Exercise Science. She is gregarious, a former college athlete, and loves the outdoors.

BOB: A successful businessman. He's rather conservative in his religious and moral outlook. He has attended the Aspen Institute for several summers and is hooked on "philosophy and the mountains."

MARK: Bob's younger friend. Mark does legal work for Bob's business. They golf together. He is sympathetic to an ethics of self-interest.

ALICE: Works in the public school system. She is also pursuing a Ph.D. in Educational Administration.

ANTHONY: A government employee. Anthony is black, interested in local politics, and is married to Alice.

DONOVAN: The stranger. A mysterious figure who apparently lives by himself in the mountains. He appears at the campsite intermittently. He knows Peter.

Dialogue One:
What Is Ethics?

The setting for these dialogues is a backpacking expedition sponsored by the Department of Health, Physical Education, and Recreation at the local university. The department sponsors various outdoor activities for faculty, staff, and alumni. All of the characters in these dialogues have some relation to the university, either as former or as current students or, in the case of Peter, as a current faculty member. The first dialogue takes place on the evening of the first day of hiking. The guides have wisely limited the initial hiking distance so the group won't tire too quickly. All of the parties, feeling energized by the crisp mountain air and the beautiful surroundings, are interested in conversing. They have set up camp and have prepared the evening meal. The fire is crackling. The guides initiate the first night's discussion by asking the campers to introduce themselves briefly and to say something about their jobs, interests, or goals.

RANSOM: Could I have your attention for a second? [Pause.] I know we've all met informally, but why don't we go around the camp fire and introduce ourselves. Say a little something about what we do and what we're interested in.

SARAH: I'll start. I'm not shy! I'm Sarah, I go to school at the university, where I'm working for a Master's in Exercise Science. I played basketball in college. I love to party, and I love to shop! This is the fourth time I've been a guide on one of these backpacking trips.

RANSOM: I'm Ransom. I'm also working on a Master's degree, but in Recreation Studies. I love the outdoors, and I hope to get a job somewhere as a recreation director.

SOPHIA: Hello. My name is Sophia, and I'm a minister at the First Unitarian Church. I decided to do this because I'm interested in wilderness concerns and ecological issues and I wanted some firsthand experience to stimulate my interests.

ROSE: My name is Rose. I have four wonderful children, and I can't believe I let my old friend Sophia talk me into this crazy adventure. She's been pulling these stunts since we were in high school.

BOB: I'm Bob. I've been in the furniture and appliance business for twenty-five years. The last three summers I went to the Aspen Institute in Colorado, and I find I can't get enough of the mountains now. Also, I'd say my experience at Aspen caused me to be very interested in philosophy—as a kind of hobby.

MARK: My name is Mark, and I feel a little like Rose. My golfing friend here, Bob, somehow talked me into this trip, and right now my feet hurt. I'm a lawyer, I like nice cars, fine wine, excellent cuisine, and I'm interested in the market.

ALICE: Alice. I'm a curriculum specialist in the public school system, and I'm also pursuing a doctorate in Educational Administration. This gentleman to my right, who happens to be my husband, thought we needed to get out of the city for a while. Here we are.

ANTHONY: My name is Anthony. I work for the State Highway Department. I'm interested in politics, and I've been actively involved in some recent minority political concerns in our community.

PETER: I'm Peter. [He speaks with a heavy English accent.] I teach at the university and, like Sophia, I suppose this trip has a certain connection with my interests in the wilderness and a more primitive relation to the natural world.

SARAH: What do you do, Professor? I mean, what do you teach exactly?

PETER: Please call me Peter. I teach in the Department of Philosophy.

BOB: Do you! As I said, I've become very interested in philosophy. Do you know Mortimer Adler's work?

PETER: Yes, I'm familiar with some of his writing.

SARAH: So, Peter, are you going to prove the mountains are an illusion?

PETER: [Smiling.] Actually, I'm only here to prove that I can benefit from a nice vacation.

ANTHONY: Well, you must admit, Professor—I mean, Peter— that you have one of those professions that's liable to stop a conversation before it gets started.

PETER: Do you think so? Look at Bob here. He mentioned his recently developed interest in philosophy. Teaching philosophy, I admit, is not for everybody. But I've often found that people take a lively interest in the fact that I'm a philosopher. I've always believed that everybody is already involved, somehow, in philosophy.

ALICE: Really? Why would you say that, Peter?

PETER: Quite simply, philosophy addresses important issues about human life.

SARAH: Yeah, like the fact of human suffering. There is nothing like a course in philosophy to make somebody suffer. I remember it well. Sophomore year, 8:30 in the morning. My brain is on hold that early. And all that heavy thinking. Whew! I was glad to get a "C."

SOPHIA: Seriously, Peter, tell us more. I've dabbled a little in philosophy. What important issues do you have in mind?

PETER: Questions of God, evil, freedom, human nature, politics, aesthetic value, morality. My main interest is ethics.

RANSOM: I'm like Sarah. I remember taking a philosophy course. Actually, it was an ethics course. We talked about all kinds of moral problems and theories. Lots of interesting discussion, but we didn't get anywhere. I've forgotten all of the theoretical stuff. Come to think of it, it was kind of hard to figure out what ethics was.

SOPHIA: So you're a moral philosopher! That's fascinating. One of the reasons I decided to come on this backpacking trip was because of some of the reading I've been doing on environmental ethics. I prepared a sermon on Albert Schweitzer some weeks ago. Do you know his work?

PETER: Scarcely.

SOPHIA: He believes the basis of ethics is a reverence for all life. He sees a kind of mystical unity in all life, and if we see ourselves as part of this unity we should also recognize and respect life in other forms—in all forms.

SARAH: In all forms?

SOPHIA: Yes.

ROSE: It sounds like a lovely ideal.

MARK: Yes, that's what it sounds like, an ideal that sounds good, but it's unrealistic.

SOPHIA: I'm not so sure about that. Albert Schweitzer was a kind of saint. Do you know anything about his life? A great theologian and scholar, a master of playing the organ—and even building organs—and then he devoted his life as a medical doctor to tribal people in Africa.

MARK: That's wonderful. But all people can't be like Schweitzer. And his so-called "ethic" isn't going to work in the real world. He doesn't really mean that we ought to be concerned about insects, does he? Look. There's an ant. [He rises, and steps on the ant.] Is that wrong?

SOPHIA: You find it silly to think that we should be concerned about a little ant? That ant is alive, it does things to sustain itself, it's part of a larger whole, an ecological whole, an organism that we're a part of. You had no reason to step on that ant. Why not let it live? Why not develop an attitude that respects it and the ecological web it's a part of? Your attitude is just the kind of view that has caused so many of our problems. You see humans at the center of things and if something isn't useful or valuable to humans, then— smash it! It can't be of any value at all. I don't accept that. Not only do I not accept it, I think the clash between your human-centered ethic and some broader ecological ethic may be one of the central issues facing us as we go into the twenty-first century.

MARK: Look, I'm saying this. You may say we should "revere" life or respect it, but you can't live consistently with that as a principle. Here's an example. We were told to bring water purification tablets. Why? To kill bacteria! How could Schweitzer be a doctor and "revere" all life? He was committed to wiping out disease, wasn't he? Didn't he have to kill viruses? Bacteria? Respect all life? What if we didn't cut down trees? Or pull weeds? Anyway, ethics involves people, doesn't it Peter?

SOPHIA: Can I respond? Even Schweitzer realized that sometimes it might be necessary to injure or harm some kind of life, for some greater value. I think he's saying that we should start with this fundamental attitude of reverence, and then reflect on difficult decisions where reverence for life might lead to some injury or harm.

BOB: I'd like to hear our philosopher respond to Mark's question. Isn't ethics about how we treat people? Isn't it about *human* values?

SARAH: I'd still like to hear a definition of ethics.

PETER: Oh, I suspect that if we think about it for a while, we could come up with a definition, especially since we have the help of Ransom, here, who has taken an ethics course.

RANSOM: That's not fair, Peter. Here you're the expert and you want me to define ethics?

BOB: Careful, people, do you remember Socrates and his style? Answer a question with a question. These philosophers are crafty people. Hard to pin down. That's the way they're taught. Always more and more questions.

RANSOM: Sounds like a game without an end, but I'll play along. Maybe I can get some help from the group here.

ANTHONY: Ethics has to do with values doesn't it?

SARAH: It has to do with what society expects us to do. As Mark said, it probably involves the human values that society teaches us. Like the fact that it's all right to kill insects.

ALICE: Sounds good to me. Social ethics is an important part of educational development. Let's say ethics is what society expects of us. *It's society's expectation about what we should value.* How's that, Peter?

PETER: Well, it's a start. I think your definition has some attractive features. We normally think of the ethical, in a broad sense, as involving us socially and as concerning values. But . . .

BOB: See? Here it comes. The dialectical hatchet begins to fall.

ROSE: The what? [Turns to Sophia.] What's he talking about?

SOPHIA: Intellectual talk Bob learned at the Aspen Institute.

PETER: Forgive me. At any rate, although it's attractive, your definition seems too broad. Surely ethics has something essentially to do with values, but that definition embraces more than we really want to include in the ethical arena. Can you see why?

BOB: Probably because so-called ethical values are not the only kind of values. Mark spoke of human values, but that's a little vague.

PETER: I can see that Bob may know how to play this philosophical game. That's it precisely. Surely not all values are the concern of ethics. Perhaps I can make the point by expressing the following: All ethical statements or moral statements (and, for now, I'll use these terms interchangeably) are value statements, but not all value statements are ethical statements. Think about this for a moment, and you'll begin to see that your definition is too broad.

MARK: I see that. It's like saying that while all reptiles are animals, not all animals are reptiles. One group is a subset of another. What you mean is that the term "values" refers to a broader category than does "ethics" or "morals."

PETER: Yes. Can anyone give an example of a value statement that is not an ethical or moral statement?

SOPHIA: I suppose aesthetic judgments, like "The mountains are beautiful," would be value judgments.

PETER: Surely. It's about the value of something being beautiful as opposed to being ugly.

SARAH: How about something like "You've set the tent up correctly"? Or better, "Air Jordan is a great basketball player."

MARK: How about this? "We ought to spray for cockroaches."

PETER: [Smiling.] Very good. There are different value judgments that belong to different fields of value studies and different areas of our experience. There are religious values, political values, aesthetic values, personal values, and something we normally call ethical or moral values.

MARK: Fine, but what is a value?

PETER: What do *you* think? We sometimes speak, positively or negatively, of someone's values. We make value judgments all the time. What do you think we're doing when we make value judgments?

SOPHIA: Well, I find it of great value to leave the city and experience these majestic mountains. I find friendship of great value. That's why Rose and I have remained close for so many years. Values have to do with what we want in life. The things that guide our life and make life worthwhile.

PETER: Quite nice. That's the basic idea. Values, in a positive sense, are goods, aren't they? They are things we like or desire. In fact, some philosophers define "goodness" as desirability, as if "the good is the object of desire."

SOPHIA: But doesn't this lead to something questionable? If ethics involves values and values involve what we desire or want, then ethics is personal. I don't like what you like; I don't act necessarily the way you or society wants me to act. If a value judgment is just a personal expression of what I like or don't like, or what I approve or don't approve of, ethics is just a matter of personal taste.

BOB: In my view, ethics is surely *not* just a matter of personal taste. You can't tell me that being cruel to another human being is just a matter of personal taste. If you have sadistic desires, that's wrong.

PETER: Let's try to unpack a few things. This is getting philosophically interesting. May I offer a few hints?

ROSE: Please offer more than a few. I'm lost.

PETER: We'll, it's important to know that value judgments are only one realm of human discourse. There is also a realm of non-evaluative statements, since they merely report facts and do not express a commitment to a value. Notice that, in this sense, so-called descriptive statements are "impersonal," since they're not a matter of expressing likes and dislikes. Statements such as "Water is composed of hydrogen and oxygen" and "The earth is the third planet from the sun in our solar system" are obvious examples of descriptive or nonevaluative statements. Now, this is a terribly knotty issue and one widely discussed in moral philosophy, but ethical statements, as evaluative, are often taken to be what philosophers call *prescriptive* statements. If I say "you ought to set up the tent in such and such a manner," then I am making a prescriptive claim. One way we might identify the ethical is to consider the different kinds of prescriptive claims we make.

SARAH: What has this to do with personal expressions of approval or disapproval? That's what we said value statements are.

PETER: If you tell me that I ought to set up the tent in a certain manner, you are recommending a course of action and you seem to be both expressing your approval and wanting me also to approve and act accordingly. You're saying it's a good way to set up the tent and I ought to choose to set it up that way. So there is something personal about such statements since I have to choose a certain course of action. What I want to know now is this: How can we distinguish those prescriptive claims that we would call ethical and moral from other types of prescriptive claims in which I also have to make a choice? Give me an example of an ought statement that is not ethical or moral.

MARK: The one you just mentioned about the tent. That's not an ethical statement.

PETER: Are you sure? Others?

SOPHIA: No, that's not ethical. It's a matter of having a purpose and knowing what is the most practical way to get the job done.

SARAH: How about this: Everyone should work out regularly for health reasons. That's not ethical.

PETER: I agree. That's what might be called a matter of prudence or self-interest. It makes good sense to work out since health is important for life. If these prescriptions aren't ethical, give me a prescriptive statement that *is* ethical.

BOB: The one I mentioned before. It's wrong to be cruel to other human beings.

MARK: Where's the "ought"?

BOB: It's there. It's assumed. Being cruel to others is morally wrong; it's just not right, so we ought not to be cruel.

PETER: Excellent. The ethical has something to do with saying that certain actions are right or wrong, or that we ought or ought not to do certain things—but again, in a more specific sense. From the examples so far, it seems that ethical or moral statements are not just statements about what's in our self-interest or what is the best way to achieve our goals. How about some other oughts? How about "One ought not to eat mashed potatoes with one's fingers"? Is that a moral statement?

ROSE: That's simply good manners.

SOPHIA: Etiquette. It's etiquette.

ANTHONY: The ethical is more important than that. When I think of ethics or morals, I think of justice and the way blacks and other minorities have been mistreated in this country.

ALICE: What about abortion rights? That's an ethical issue.

BOB: I would ask, what about the rights of the fetus?

MARK: These are legal and constitutional questions, aren't they?

SOPHIA: But what about stopping at a stop sign? That's a matter of law. But that's not an ethical matter, is it?

SARAH: I've got one. In basketball, I don't think you ought to taunt your opponent, like those players who yell "In your face!" when they make a basket. Or what about adolescent behavior in tennis? I don't think somebody ought to act like a jerk all of the time. Are these ethical statements?

PETER: What do *you* think?

SOPHIA: I have some more controversial examples. I happen to think that any kind of sexual behavior between or *among* consenting adults is a matter of personal taste and not a *moral* issue at all, as some seem to think. In fact, I wish some people would get their moral noses out of other people's private affairs.

BOB: But when that behavior is unnatural and threatens the moral fabric of society, when the family is endangered, we as a society cannot tolerate it.

MARK: I have to agree with Bob on that.

PETER: I must say, it's striking that matters of value are things people really care about. That's one of the reasons I think philosophy is important. It attempts to think hard about these matters. Although there is disagreement among us, let's see if our disagreement helps us illuminate the ethical sphere. Take the ought statements that are *clearly* moral or ethical versus those that are obviously *not* involved with ethical matters. What's the difference?

ANTHONY: Remember my example. Our country has a history associated with slavery, discrimination, and injustice. People have not been treated fairly, and they continue to suffer from discrimination and racism. As opposed to eating mashed potatoes with your fingers or getting enough exercise, people have been hurt. Matters of etiquette, at least, seem trivial in the face of pervasive injustice.

BOB: My example of cruelty suggests the same thing. When people are hurt for no reason, that's morally reprehensible.

SOPHIA: And that is precisely why I'm inclined to believe that voluntary sexual matters are ethically permissible, although I recognize there is disagreement. But it strikes me that my disagreement with Bob is partly a matter of whether society is hurt by such behavior. If it is, then I would agree that people ought not to do kinky or weird sexual things. But I don't believe that happens.

PETER: Not bad. Many philosophers believe that ethical reflection essentially involves considering the ways in which one's actions affect others—as if, when I act with ethical or moral considerations in mind, I must consider not only myself, but I must also consider the interests of others. Some hold that morality involves considering the interests of others as equal to one's own, that is, acting on rules or principles that embody this consideration of others. Think of the great moral principle we're often taught when we're young.

RANSOM: "Do unto others as you would have them do unto you."

ROSE: That's a principle I've tried very hard to teach my children.

PETER: I believe it's at least one profound expression of "the moral point of view."

RANSOM: But what does this do to our original definition?

PETER: We began by suggesting that ethics involves values. Now we are in a position to make a more specific and enlightening suggestion. Ethics appears to involve values that guide our life and conduct from a particular perspective. We are often asked in life to behave in such a way that we do not act solely in terms of self-interest and that we consider others' interests as important in making our decision. Some philosophers would put it this way. Sometimes there are situations in life where there is a conflict between what we *want* to do and what we think we *ought* to do, between self-interest and duty. The moral point of view appears to involve our sense that we have duties or obligations. That the *right* thing to do from the moral point of view is sometimes contrary to a simple calculation of doing what's best for us personally or what will give us the most pleasure. Think of Alice's and Anthony's examples. Southern slave holders made huge profits by enslaving blacks. The white minority in South Africa is assured of a more comfortable life as long as apartheid remains. But slavery and apartheid are morally pernicious. They're morally wrong, period.

ROSE: Peter, let me offer my own example of what you're saying. My oldest son promised a friend he would help him clean a vacant lot one Saturday. The night before, another friend called and offered him free football tickets to a big football game the next day. He wanted to back out of the work. We talked, and I told him that he gave his word and it would be wrong to break it. Plus, his friend needed his help.

SOPHIA: She's always been a wonderful influence on her children and a wonderful mother. And a wonderful friend.

ROSE: I've just always felt that it's important to be sensitive to others, to know how they feel. I've tried to teach that to my children.

PETER: Doesn't this show us something else interesting about moral situations? Rose wanted her son to do the right thing and thought there were good reasons for him to help his friend. He made a promise and he should keep it, and she believed he would somehow hurt another person if he didn't keep his word. He had two powerful *moral* reasons to help his friend, and his own pleasure, what he wanted to do, was judged to be less important than the moral values involved.

SARAH: But what if, say, a family member had needed Rose's son that day? Or what if another friend had gotten in trouble and needed his help? What then?

PETER: Then the process of moral decision making would have been more difficult, as it often is.

BOB: Ransom still wants us to relate what we have been talking about to the original definition. Right?

RANSOM: Right. As I recall, we started by attempting to define ethics in terms of society's expectations concerning what we should value.

PETER: I fear I'll have to muddy the water somewhat, but we now need to make an important distinction or two.

BOB: Go ahead. I find this fascinating.

PETER: So far, I've used the terms "ethics" and "morality" interchangeably, but there are important reasons to be careful about our usage of these terms and their derivatives. Remember our original reference to the expectations of society. Clearly, ethics in some way involves our social life, but does it amount to a simple allegiance to what society expects of us? Surely ethics is more challenging than that. In fact, philosophers are often careful to separate ethics from what they call "morals" precisely on the grounds that, while they both consider the same type of value, "morals" is uncritical, whereas ethics is a critical examination of the issues involved. In a word, ethics is philosophical, whereas morals need not be. This is at least one way to distinguish "ethics" and "morality." Ethics doesn't take for granted what society expects or happens to hold as moral. Ethics asks you to think for yourself. On the basis of this, we can at least say that ethics is the philosophical examination of morality.

SOPHIA: When you say ethics is philosophical, what do you mean?

PETER: First of all, I mean that ethics doesn't just describe what is taken to be moral in a given context. It's not like sociology or history. It doesn't attempt to explain why some people have the moral beliefs they do. Again, this might be studied in one of the social sciences, such as psychology. Even biologists, at least sociobiologists, are interested in showing the way in which our moral desires or feelings might be explained as products of our evolutionary development.

SOPHIA: I've read some sociobiology. Very interesting.

PETER: But philosophers ask different sorts of questions in critically examining morality. What is morality? Why do we have it? What is it to make a moral judgment? Notice that we have been *doing* some philosophy, since we have been examining these issues. What is the basis for moral judgments? Are they objective? Subjective? Why should we be moral? And, especially for our present purposes, focusing on the sense in which individuals are confronted with ethically different situations, what is it to *be* moral? And what *is taken* to be moral by society may not *be* moral. That's why ethical reflection is critical and independent. It asks you not to follow unthinkingly society's values. Ethics challenges one to reflect critically on social expectations, taking nothing at face value. But I'm talking too much.

SOPHIA: No, no, not at all. I find this all very interesting. I'm sure others do also. Let me see if I have this straight. First, ethics as a value discipline is in some sense personal. Furthermore, since moral judgments don't just describe things, they *prescribe*, right? They say what we ought to do, they express our personal desire or aversion for doing certain things—that is to say, they call upon us to commit ourselves. Second, ethics is critical and independent, philosophical as you say. It rationally examines morality. Let's see . . .

MARK: And ethics considers only certain types of values, especially values that affect the way we act toward others. So ethics is a personal and philosophical examination of the value of our behavior.

PETER: Not bad, not bad at all.

BOB: One thing concerns me, however.

PETER: Yes.

BOB: I mean the emphasis on ethics as being independent and personal. If someone who seriously engages in ethical reflection doesn't necessarily accept society's values, then he is somebody who answers only to himself.

SARAH: I don't see the problem. We're all individuals. What's right for me isn't necessarily right for you.

BOB: But doesn't that make our personal ethical judgments subjective or arbitrary? This whole issue of the personal character of ethics is a problem.

PETER: [Smiles.] I wish I could pack all of you up and install you in my ethics course each term. Really good question. Let's think a little more about the "personal" character of ethics. We have to be very careful here. In what sense have we said so far that ethics is personal?

SOPHIA: Ethics is personal because in value judgments we don't just describe things impersonally. We commit ourselves.

ANTHONY: And in ethics we don't just accept society's standards. Each one of us must think for himself.

ALICE: Or *herself.*

ANTHONY: Sorry.

BOB: But ethical judgments can't be strictly personal in one sense. We've said that the moral point of view asks us to consider others, not just ourselves. Remember, "Do unto others . . ."

ROSE: That's right. Be sensitive to others; don't just think about yourself.

PETER: So there must be a sense in which ethical judgment is deeply impersonal. Philosophers sometimes insist that ethical judgment requires *impartiality* because, from the moral point of view, I must consider the interests of others as equal to my own. For example, if I have a right not to be subjected to unnecessary suffering, then other beings, insofar as they are like me, also have that same right. That is, I must to some extent judge things impartially when I think ethically.

BOB: So the personal character of ethics doesn't condemn it to being subjective or arbitrary.

PETER: No, I don't think so. This point has to do with the nature of moral reasoning and the kinds of principles we refer to when we attempt to reflect ethically.

SARAH: But I think it is subjective. No one has the right to tell me what I have to do. I still say that what is right for me isn't necessarily right for you.

PETER: I believe there's something true in what you say, but there is also something terribly misleading in your statement. Suppose you promise to meet me at 6:00 P.M. and you fail to keep the appointment, for no apparent reason. Later I become upset at you because you failed to keep your promise. I think you are untrustworthy. Now suppose a similar situation happens tomorrow, except that I promise to meet you at 6:00 P.M. and *I* fail to show up for no apparent reason. What could I say? Well, what's right for me isn't necessarily right for you. What would you say?

MARK: I know what I'd say. Who do you think you are? You're doing the same thing you criticized me for yesterday. That's just plain inconsistent.

SARAH: But what if you had something else important to do so you couldn't meet me?

PETER: Then the situations wouldn't be the same. Based on this example, it appears that from the standpoint of mere consistency we are required to make the same ethical judgments for *everyone* in similar situations. Philosophers sometimes call this *universalizability*. The relevant moral principles apply to each of us equally, so when different individuals are faced with similar situations, there is an important sense in which what is right for me is also right for you.

SARAH: I'll have to think about that. But you said you thought there was something true about my statement.

PETER: I mean this. Our lives are sometimes very different, and our moral rules and principles implicate us in different ways. For example, some think that the basic requirement in morality is to bring as much good into the world as one can. If our abilities and interests are quite different, then the moral consequences of this quite general principle would mean that what is morally required of me might be different from what is morally required of you. For example, we might be faced with different opportunities to promote goodness.

ANTHONY: But, Peter, you did say that in ethics we have to make up our own minds. No one can make my decisions for me. Doesn't that still make ethics subjective?

BOB: And arbitrary?

PETER: Good question. My reply is that ethics is indeed subjective, to a degree, but I don't think it has to be arbitrary. You see, independence of mind, using your own judgment, and having your own perspective—none of these necessarily implies arbitrariness. In other words, ethics need not be arbitrary so long as it is not completely subjective. As long as there are moral rules and principles to appeal to in moral reasoning, ethics is not completely subjective. I would argue that a sound understanding of ethics would insist on a significant measure of objectivity in judgments. Perhaps one way that I can make my point more clearly is to take an example from one of my newly developed passions—that great American pastime, baseball.

SARAH: Now we're talking.

RANSOM: Control yourself. Go ahead, Peter.

PETER: Let's take the case of the umpire. He has a right to "call 'em as he sees 'em," correct?

SARAH: Even the blind ones insist on that.

PETER: At the same time, you expect his calls to be accurate. Even if his calls are in some sense subjective or personal, they are not arbitrary. There is an objective standard—that is, a measurement not exclusively his, nor ours, but everybody's—to assess the correctness of his calls. I'm referring, of course, to the strike zone, mainly. But I dare say that for every other call in baseball there is a standard of correctness.

SARAH: But the arguments. Just look at the arguments. Rhubarbs!

PETER: Let's focus on strikes and balls. His judgment—calling a strike or a ball—is supposed to answer to what reason and evidence demands, that is, according to something objective. Quite simply, was the ball in the strike zone or out of it? This question makes sense because there is an objective standard for accuracy that is a check on the risk of pure arbitrariness on the part of the umpire. True enough, his own perspective is going to be a factor in the correctness of his call. That's why arguments occur. Fortunately, however, there is another factor involved—whether his call is reasonable in light of the evidence (where the pitch was thrown) and in light of the given standard (the strike zone).

BOB: Very suggestive. So for you, personal judgments in ethics are similar to the calls of umpires.

PETER: Something like that. Sometimes the ball is down the middle, waist high. The judgment is obvious and no one disagrees.

BOB: Like cruelty for no reason.

ANTHONY: Or slavery.

SOPHIA: Or rape.

MARK: Or murder.

PETER: Sometimes the ball is near the corner, low, moving erratically. The umpire must make a difficult call.

SOPHIA: Like abortion.

ROSE: Or euthanasia. My friend's father is terminally ill in the hospital, hooked up to all sorts of things. It's a terrible, difficult situation.

PETER: Because ethics involves personal commitment to certain issues, ethics is somewhat subjective, as you say. It entails perspective. But if ethics is genuinely philosophical, it must also appeal to reason and evidence to validate its judgments. Consider Rose's example. We must get the facts straight about the illness in question. Is there a medical chance of recovery? But then we must weigh such values as autonomy, the reduction of suffering, and the value of life itself.

ROSE: How can we be sure what to do? How do we know what the right thing is?

PETER: Centuries ago, Aristotle was convinced that ethics does appeal to reason and evidence, as we've said. But he asked to what extent ethics attains scientific objectivity. He answered that it is a science, although an inexact one. He argued that while it strives for conclusions defended by reason and experience (which makes it a kind of science), it is nonetheless limited by the nature of its subject matter, the lives of human beings. Because human experience is so varied and ambiguous, no science of human affairs can hope to be exact or altogether free of controversy. It will commonly invite different responses from different points of view.

SOPHIA: So very true. Just look at us.

PETER: Aristotle thought that you can only expect so much certainty from a study as its subject matter will allow. In other words, don't expect mathematical certainty from serious ethical reflection. Ethics has to live with a certain imprecision. But if someone tried to keep this inexactitude to a minimum, if she tries, as far as possible, to let objective, dispassionate, disinterested standards of reasoning and experience dictate her judgments, she has a right to claim that her conclusions are philosophically sound and free of arbitrariness. She has a right, rationally, to believe her conclusions.

ALICE: So ethics can be very personal and the result of independent thought, without condemning it to the privacy of our individual perspectives.

PETER: Yes, I believe that is the case.

BOB: So where are we? Can we sum this up? What is ethics, Peter? You can give us your definition.

PETER: There is a very old and very traditional definition that seems to me to succeed pretty well. It's this: *Ethics is the philosophical examination of what constitutes morally good and morally bad conduct.* Ethics focuses on the moral value of human conduct, and in this way it differs from other value subjects. It also takes into account two necessary elements of a sound definition of ethics: (1) that it is philosophical, that is, a rational or critical examination of the ultimate reasons or principles regarding human conduct; and (2) that it is concerned with the value (the desirability or undesirability) of conduct. Since it is a values discipline, personal judgments are implied. But insofar as reason and evidence are used, and since moral reasons typically articulate some degree of concern for others, there is also a significant sense in which ethics is *impersonal*, or *impartial*. In fact, in my understanding, the notion of good and bad conduct is typically understood in terms of the moral point of view, or that point of view from which we attempt to consider how our actions affect the lives of other morally significant beings. This definition also has the virtue of telling us what ethics is not, for, according to this formulation, ethics is clearly distinguished from morals (or *mores*), which is an uncritical acceptance, more or less, of what society teaches us regarding good and bad conduct.

MARK: I have only one remaining question. You've spoken of the ethical and the moral. We've mentioned etiquette and prudence. But what about the legal? I make my living in corporate law, and I deal with people every day who believe that the only standard setting boundaries on what a person ought to do is the civil law. Their view is that "if there ain't a law against it, it must be all right." How does one reply to this kind of thinking?

ANTHONY: Very simple. Segregation was once legally permitted in the United States, but in time people began to protest these unjust practices. There were unjust laws, and they were ethically wrong.

ALICE: You just can't equate ethics with civil law, else people who want to upset the status quo, like Martin Luther King and Mahatma Gandhi, would always be wrong.

BOB: It seems to me that ethics must exercise a higher authority of sorts, since we need to judge the soundness of the law. If ethics is indeed critical, a person can't simply accept the written laws of a society at face value. I think that's why there is such controversy surrounding such things as abortion, euthanasia, and pornography.

PETER: I suspect that as the ethical thinking of a people begins to mature and deepen, there is often a demand to change laws and customs. Sometimes it takes civil disobedience to bring to a society's attention ethical deficiencies in its civil laws. Ideally, we want our laws and ethical perspectives to coincide, but often they do not.

SARAH: Well, this has been very . . . uh . . .

SOPHIA: Philosophical.

SARAH: Yes, very heavy. But we need to start thinking about how early dawn comes in the mountains.

RANSOM: Could I say just one more thing before we all retire to our sleeping bags? I've been listening closely, and I hope you all won't take this the wrong way, but what happened to God? We're talking about how we ought to act. We were talking about values, and no one even mentioned God, from whom everything comes, and Jesus, the model for us all. Sophia, you're a minister. Don't you see what I mean?

SOPHIA: I guess you don't know much about the Unitarians. I happen to be a humanist, if you want a label.

RANSOM: There you go. That's it. All this stuff sounds to me like so much pagan, secular humanism. If you want my opinion, humanist ethics is sinful. That's what I thought when I took the ethics course at the university. It's just another way that Satan has duped man into thinking that he is sufficient unto himself, that he can live without God. But my Christian faith teaches me that this is a lie, an illusion. Right behavior is not something that human beings determine. Human life is too important for that. How human beings ought to live is dictated solely by God. What God says is right is right; what God says is wrong is wrong. You say morals and law are different from ethics. I say that ethics is unimportant compared to knowing what God commands for each of us.

PETER: Well, perhaps Ransom has assumed that there must be some conflict between ethics, as philosophical, and religion. I have difficulty with that assumption. Perhaps ethical reflection and religious morals may be quite compatible in important respects. It's just that they *approach* moral questions differently; they begin from different vantage points or starting places, if you will. Perhaps they lead to similar conclusions. It's possible that they don't differ so much in their conclusions as in their methods.

SOPHIA: Well, I've got to see this. I know I reach my ethical conclusions differently from the Bible thumpers.

ROSE: That's not very kind, Sophia.

SOPHIA: And I encourage my congregation to think for themselves. We are committed to the free and disciplined search for truth by *each* individual.

PETER: Ransom's challenge is an important one. If you're interested, we can discuss this tomorrow. For now, I want to take a brief walk and listen to the wind through the pines.

What Thinkers Have Said

Men of Athens, I honour and love you; but I shall obey God rather than you, and while I have life and strength I shall never cease from the practice and teaching of philosophy, exhorting any one whom I meet and say to him after my manner: You, my friend—a citizen of the great and mighty and wise city of Athens—are you not ashamed of heaping up the greatest amount of money and honour and reputation, and caring so little about wisdom and truth and the greatest improvement of the soul, which you never regard or heed at all? And if the person with

whom *I* am arguing, says: Yes, but *I* do care; then *I* do not leave him or let him
go at once; but *I* proceed to interrogate and examine and cross-examine him, and
if *I* think that he has no virtue in him, but only says that he has, *I* reproach him
with undervaluing the greater, and overvaluing the less.

Plato, *Apology*

We must therefore examine whether we should act in this way or not, as not
only now but at all times I am the kind of man who listens only to the argument
that on reflection seems best to me.

Plato, *Crito*

We must be content, then, in speaking of such subjects and with such premises
to indicate the truth roughly and in outline, and in speaking about things which
are only for the most part true and with premises of the same kind to reach
conclusions that are no better. In the same spirit, therefore, should each type of
statement be received; for it is the mark of an educated man to look for precision
in each class of things just so far as the nature of the subject admits; it is evidently
equally foolish to accept probable reasoning from a mathematician and to demand
from a rhetorician scientific proofs.

Aristotle, *Nichomachean Ethics*

Thus anthropology observes the actual behavior of human beings and formu-
lates the practical and subjective rules which that behaviour obeys, whereas moral
philosophy alone seeks to formulate rules of right conduct, that is, of what ought
to happen, just as logic comprises the rules for the right use of the mind. When
we say that something ought to be, we mean that a possible action is capable of
being good, it comprises rules for the proper use of the will.

Immanuel Kant, *Lectures on Ethics*

The intellectual distinction between customary and reflective morality is clearly
marked. The former places the standard and rules of conduct in ancestral habit;
the latter appeals to conscience, reason, or to some principle which includes
thought. The distinction is as important as it is definite, for it shifts the center of
gravity in morality, Nevertheless the distinction is relative rather than absolute.
Some degree of reflective thought must have entered occasionally into systems
which in the main were founded on social wont and use, while in contemporary
morals, even when the need of critical judgment is most recognized, there is an
immense amount of conduct that is merely accommodated to social usage.

John Dewey, *Theory of the Moral Life*

The very raison d'être of a morality is to yield reasons which overrule the reasons *of self-interest in those cases when everyone's following self-interest would be harmful to everyone. Hence moral reasons are superior to all others.*

Kurt Baier, *The Moral Point of View*

It is not a trivial question, Socrates said: what we are talking about is how one should live. Or so Plato reports him, in one of the first books written about this subject. Plato thought that philosophy could answer the question. Like Socrates, he hoped that one could direct one's life, if necessary redirect it, through an understanding that was distinctively philosophical—that is to say, general and abstract, rationally reflective, and concerned with what can be known through different kinds of inquiry.

The aims of moral philosophy, and any hopes it may have of being worth serious attention, are bound up with the fate of Socrates' question, even if it is not true that philosophy, itself, can reasonably hope to answer it.

Bernard Williams, *Ethics and the Limits of Philosophy*

Key Terms and Concepts

values	moral reasons
ethics	impartiality
morals	objectivity of ethics
descriptive	subjectivity of ethics
prescriptive	morality and legality
moral point of view	

Questions

1. How would you define morality?

2. Describe a situation in which you have faced a *moral* problem or dilemma. Why do you think the situation is a "moral" one? What did you do? How did you decide what to do?

3. Give examples of judgments or situations that are indisputably moral and uncontroversially nonmoral. (You might assume that the entire class would have to agree with your example. Also, be careful. The question is whether a judgment or situation has *some* moral significance, not whether it is moral as opposed to immoral.) Now give examples of situations or judgments that have disputable moral significance. On the basis of your examples, what can you conclude about the nature of the moral as opposed to the nonmoral? Do your conclusions agree with the points made in the dialogue?

4. Why do we have morality? What is the purpose or function of morality? Does morality perhaps have more than one purpose?

5. Although it may be a bit premature to consider the question, you might consider what some believe to be *the* great philosophical question associated with morality: Why be moral?

6. Explain how the following distinctions relate to the attempt in the dialogue to clarify the nature of ethics: fact-value, descriptive-prescriptive, personal-impersonal, self-interest-impartiality, subjective-objective, ethics-morals, critical-uncritical.

7. Explain the way in which the baseball analogy exemplifies the nature of moral reasoning. Can you think of other analogies that might be as revealing?

Suggested Readings

Aristotle, *Nicomachean Ethics*, in *The Basic Works of Aristotle*, Richard McKeon, ed., Random House, 1941.

Baier, Kurt, *The Moral Point of View*, Random House, 1965.

Dewey, John, *Theory of the Moral Life,* Holt, Rinehart, and Winston, 1960.

Frankena, William K., *Ethics,* 2nd ed., Prentice-Hall, 1973. A widely used introductory treatment of many of the issues discussed in this book. He defends his own ethical theory, which combines utilitarianism and deontology.

Hospers, John, *Human Conduct: Problems of Ethics,* 2nd ed., Harcourt Brace Jovanovich, Inc., 1982. Extensive treatment of the problems of ethics; many helpful exercises at the end of each chapter.

Johnson, Oliver, ed., *Ethics: Selections from Classical and Contemporary Writers,* 4th ed., Holt, Rinehart, and Winston, 1978. An excellent collection of central readings from the history of ethics.

Kant, Immanuel, *Lectures on Ethics,* trans. by Louis Infield, Harper and Row, 1963.

Plato, *The Trial and Death of Socrates,* trans. by G. M. A. Grube, Hackett Publishing Co., 1975. A rich literary and philosophical expression of Socrates' mature moral thought.

Rachels, James, *The Elements of Moral Philosophy,* Random House, 1986. Especially clear and brief introduction of ethics.

Singer, Peter, *Practical Ethics,* Cambridge University Press, 1979. "About Ethics," the first chapter, is a helpful account of what ethics is and is not.

Taylor, Paul, *Principles of Ethics,* Dickenson, 1975. Good overview of the various ethical theories with sufficient attention given to the history of ethics.

Williams, Bernard, *Ethics and the Limits of Philosophy,* Harvard University Press, 1985.

Dialogue Two:
Ethics and Religion

At the end of the second day, a few of the backpackers have again gathered around the camp fire. Bob, a lover of philosophical conversation, is eager to continue the previous night's discussion.

Ransom continues to doubt that moral thinking can be valid if separated from religion. He argues that the only sure guide to moral choice is divine revelation, specifically Christianity. Peter explains that Ransom's position is a version of what philosophers call "Divine Command Theory." Peter and the others subject this theory to criticism. In particular, Peter argues that ethics is an autonomous sphere of human reasoning, independent from religious commitments.

BOB: So, Ransom, should we see what the professor has to say about your comments last night?

RANSOM: Oh, it's all right. I don't want to bore people with my own personal views. I'm not sure that anyone wants to go on with what we did last night.

SOPHIA: On the contrary, I thought we had a stimulating discussion.

BOB: And we've got the good professor here—a philosopher at that. I can't turn down a chance like this, to talk to a professional philosopher. And here I thought I was only paying for the chance to be in the mountains!

SARAH: Come on, Reverend Ransom, let's see what Peter has to say.

RANSOM: Well, Peter?

PETER: Please, go ahead.

RANSOM: It just struck me last night, as we were talking, that even way out here the world is full of secular humanism. Our pastor's last sermon before I came on this trip was about the damaging effects of secular humanism on the modern world.

PETER: I must say, Ransom, that is one of those expressions people use when they want to lash out at an idea they're not comfortable with. I find the phrase rather vague, so vague, in fact, as to mean nothing unless you clarify it for me. Could you tell me what you mean by the term "secular humanism"?

RANSOM: Yes, I think so. It's fairly simple. I mean a belief that I've found all too common among college intellectual types. And I heard it last night, that the meaning of human life can be understood by the human mind alone—I mean, without the help of God. Secular humanists believe that human beings on their own can make sense of their own experiences, and require no aid from God for an explanation of the significance and purpose of their lives.

SOPHIA: Do you mean any thinking that doesn't include God? What about science?

RANSOM: If science is done without seeing the world as the creation of God, then it is a form of secular humanism. But I mean especially the thinking that involves the purpose for which we're here and what we're supposed to do with our lives as gifts from God.

BOB: You seem to think that philosophy itself is an expression of secular humanism.

RANSOM: That's what Peter said last night. Ethical thinking is independent and critical, as if we must ignore the will of God when we make ethical decisions.

PETER: Let's reflect for a moment on what you're saying. Suppose it *is* the case that, in some ultimate sense, religion is required to explain the purpose of human life. That, of course, is a large assumption for some people, and they will protest.

SOPHIA: You bet they will. Many people who go to my church want nothing to do with traditional religion. They might believe that "religion" in a very broad sense, is important in life, but they reject the traditional theism of the Judeo-Christian tradition. Are we talking about religion, or are we talking about theistic religion?

RANSOM: I'm talking about faith in God and the purpose of human life.

PETER: Let us, for the sake of our discussion, consider the implications of Ransom's Christian theism.

SARAH: What do you mean by theism?

PETER: Simply, the belief in a personal being, infinitely powerful and good, who exists *above* or *outside* of nature. That's why classical theism is a form of supernaturalism. Is that satisfactory, Ransom?

RANSOM: Yes.

PETER: Then let's assume, for the sake of discussion, that theistic religion is required to explain the purpose of human life. To my mind, it still does not follow that ethics is wholly dependent on religion, or, to draw on what we've said before, that ethics is reducible to religious morals. Ethics involves the evaluation of human conduct. Why can't a person, whether religious in this sense or not, be involved in this practice?

SOPHIA: Not only why *can't* they, but why shouldn't they? I know many persons, including agnostics, atheists, pantheists, and New Age wackos who are good people. They are principled, morally upright, and I'd sure trust them more than your run-of-the-mill TV evangelist with his money-grubbing hands constantly in your pockets.

RANSOM: I'm not here to defend sinful preachers. We're all sinners.

SOPHIA: But these atheists and agnostics don't seem to find religious commitment necessary for their moral decision making. In fact, to the eyes of all with whom they come into contact, they seem to be as moral as anyone. They're sensitive to others, fair, keep their word, and tell the truth.

RANSOM: But you see what happens is that these people, these "good atheists" as you call them, are substituting their own desires and choices for the will of God in their lives. According to my religion, this is a sin, a very serious sin.

SOPHIA: Not mine. I have no use for the term "sin."

RANSOM: It is sheer human arrogance to think that sinful human beings can understand anything without God. God's creation, including the very values we've talked about, is only understood and appreciated because of the love and the wisdom of God, who, in his infinite goodness, has shared with us through divine revelation.

SOPHIA: Ransom, you recognize that many simply reject this picture of the world.

PETER: Look, we shan't agree on the larger metaphysical issue, but we can reflect on its implications, if it turns out to be true. You may be right that in some ultimate sense, or in the grand scheme of things, human lives depend on God. Maybe that is the case. Without God, perhaps there is no purpose to human life. But we'll let the existentialists worry over such matters. I'm more interested in the narrower question of whether ethics can in any sense stand on its own as a distinct or autonomous human study, even *if* your religious theism turns out to be true.

BOB: It's clear that without God, ethics must be autonomous. That's obvious. So you're pressing us to consider whether it's possible for there to be morality or ethical reflection independent of religious morals even if God exists.

PETER: Yes, and I take it that Ransom is unwilling to accept such a possibility. So he assumes that ethics, as autonomous, critical, human thinking, must be a kind of "secular humanism," to use his phrase. As if ethics is necessarily Godless and opposed to the principles of religious morals.

RANSOM: One thing Bob said I don't agree with. He says that if there's no God it's obvious that ethics must be autonomous. I'm saying, without God, there can't be ethics. [And if you do ethics without God, you are sinfully mistaken.]

BOB: I didn't mean to endorse that position. I'm a theist also. I was just trying to clarify the question at hand. So, Peter, evidently you disagree with our believer here.

PETER: Yes, I think he may be laboring under a confusion. Just because ethics relies on a different method or approach to evaluate human conduct does not mean that it is necessarily opposed to religious morals, and it is precisely for that reason that I think even nonreligious people can be sound moral thinkers and good people. While ethics is not the same as religious morals, which would base the acceptance of standards for right and wrong conduct on the basis of religious faith, the two are not necessarily opposed, at least not in principle. Ethics, relying as it does on our own *natural* understanding, suspends judgment about religious claims to *supernatural* revelation. Even many thinkers who are openly committed to Christian revelation understand this, and take self-conscious pains not to let religious presumptions be constitutive of their philosophical, or strictly ethical, argumentation.

BOB: I can endorse that point. It's true even of great Christian personalities, even saints. Take the case of Thomas Aquinas, for example. The last two or three years, I've read a lot of Aquinas's writings and I've read about him. As a philosopher, he wrote about ethics, but sometimes he wore another hat, as a theologian, a religious thinker who wrote about what we've called religious morals. He wrote about what God has communicated to people through religious tradition or revelation regarding how we ought to act. But I think Aquinas understood that, while thinking as a philosopher, about the ethical life, it was important not to use the same methods and standards that are common to the moral theologian, such as appeal to scripture, church authority, and religious tradition, to establish claims about right and wrong.

SOPHIA: How could he, as a philosopher, use theological appeals? If a philosopher wants to communicate with others who don't share certain specific religious assumptions, such appeals will fall on deaf ears.

PETER: I would say that the methods of the two, ethics and religious morals, are different and should not be confused. It is not that the philosopher or ethician aims to contradict or undermine religious morals; it is just that he is interested in an approach that suspends the question of religious commitment and relies on a "natural" as opposed to a "supernatural" or "revelatory" standard for determining the question of right and wrong. He simply strives to rely on what we all, as human beings, have in common: our own natural reason and experience; our own desires, goals, interests, and concerns; and the fact that we must live together in a common social world. There is something called moral reasoning that helps us sustain and enhance our social and individual lives.

SOPHIA: If that's true, and I think it is, the person who thinks ethically can speak, presumably, to an audience outside her own culture and religious faith. She's not arguing from some questionable presumed theology that only the elect has access to. She can appeal to the rationality and experience of anyone, regardless of culture and religion. I hear Peter saying that philosophy is just *indifferent* to religion, not opposed to it. Is that right, Peter?

PETER: Yes, quite right. Or so it seems to me.

RANSOM: But if a philosopher is "indifferent" to religion, as you say, doesn't it amount to the same thing? Won't the philosopher justify conclusions that contradict religious morals?

PETER: Not necessarily. Bob mentioned Aquinas, and quite appropriately I should think. As a philosopher, Aquinas sought to justify conclusions according to the light of natural reason. But it also happened that the conclusions he thereby justified accorded with the conclusions of religious morals. Even if one doesn't accept many of Aquinas's specific arguments, I think that there is something very instructive in his attempt to show that, while ethics and religious morals have different methods, different approaches to their subject matter, these differences do not necessarily point to contradictory conclusions. For example, consider a number of the Ten Commandments. Here is one of the greatest Christian philosophers, who appeared to think that ethics and religion need not be thought of as enemies. Again, it's just that ethics is not particularly interested in bringing God and religion into the question. It is concerned, as a discipline, only with what human beings, on their own, can discern about right and wrong.

RANSOM: But I just can't see the point to ethics if we have religious faith. God gives us all the "ethics" we need. It's dangerous and arrogant to use your "reason" to "test" what God teaches. Or to ignore what God teaches. We are created by God; we exist for God; we are meant to live according to God's law. Nothing else matters. Submission to God in all aspects of our lives is all that matters. His law is sufficient. Ethics is a human invention. It's not even necessary. And for a Christian, it's wrong to rely on a merely human enterprise, ethics, which, like everything that sinful humans do, is unsure and vague, unlike God's revelation, which we can always rely on.

SOPHIA: Ransom, Ransom. I like you; please don't take my remarks personally, but really! The first thing that strikes me is that you're in a strange position when it comes to the great social and moral issues of our day. I can understand why you might make certain personal choices, but what if you want to persuade others in a public forum? What if you're a legislator? What kind of arguments can you make? We live in a liberal democratic society in which the government is constitutionally prohibited from establishing or endorsing a particular religious point of view. If nothing else, ethics is vitally necessary for public discourse concerning the pressing moral issues of the day, like abortion and euthanasia and equality and affirmative action.

SARAH: And you keep talking about revelation, Ransom. But what about other supposed revelations? How about the Ayatollah? His revelation is that Allah wants his people to rise up against the Godless West.

PETER: Sarah's point is well-taken. One should keep in mind that any claim about revelation requires interpretation. As you know, there are many different revelations the world over. There is the Christian revelation, the Islamic revelation, the Jewish revelation, and so on. If right and wrong are purely a matter of the revealed word of God, which revelation do we appeal to?

RANSOM: Well, I simply follow the Bible on that—the Christian revelation, as spelled out in the Bible, the inspired word of God. That's the only genuine revelation.

SARAH: How do you know that? I think you say that just because you were brought up in this culture. What if you had been brought up in Iran? You'd be spouting the Koran.

SOPHIA: And what about me, Ransom? I quit believing Protestant preachers when I was in high school. But that made me search. I've been searching ever since. I want to understand Islam, and Buddhism, and Hinduism. I want to *think* about their teachings, including their ethical teachings. If they all claim to have *the* truth, I can't simply accept one just because I happen to be most familiar with it.

PETER: It is obvious that Jews and Muslims would argue about Ransom's appeal to the Christian Bible as the sole moral authority, but I don't suppose there would be much point in continuing that discussion if religious commitment was solely a matter of faith, unrelated to reason. Ransom can always argue that there is a rational basis for his Christian beliefs.

SOPHIA: That means we're back in the old ballpark of the arguments for God's existence, which is fine with me, since I don't think any of them work.

BOB: I do. I'm convinced the cosmological argument is sound.

SOPHIA: We can argue about that later. For our purposes, this attempt to make morals rely on religion means that the only way finally to justify your ethical views would be to justify your religious ones, by rational arguments, and that is notoriously difficult to do.

PETER: But the further point is telling. Even if we just limit ourselves to the Christian revelation, we have to admit that there are many distinct traditions, each espousing the preferred interpretation of Christianity. For example, do we follow the Catholic tradition or the Protestant tradition in our moral life? There *are* differences, you know.

RANSOM: The Protestant.

PETER: Recall that Luther argued that there is a "priesthood of all believers," which would, I think, lead to a variety of interpretations among even the most sincere Christians.

SOPHIA: One of my Christian friends is convinced that the correct interpretation of Jesus' teachings is that he was a pacifist. My friend is even writing a book about it. He's also a strict vegetarian, on moral grounds. That sounds pretty different from the Falwells and the Swaggarts. They want us to nuke the Godless commies!

RANSOM: I trust my pastor to help me interpret the word of God and Jesus' teachings.

SOPHIA: Well, here's another one for you. One of my favorite writers, Bertrand Russell, has some interesting things to say about moral defects in Jesus' character. I, for one, see nothing morally praiseworthy in teaching people to fear God because he might punish you eternally in the fires of hell. Especially when you're representing an infinitely loving God. I never thought that made much sense. Of course, I *did* have to think about it. And then there's what Jesus did to those poor swine, sending demons into them. I think that's cruel to the swine. Luke 8, I believe. See, I do read the Bible.

BOB: God gave us dominion over the animals. As for hell, I think it is reasonable to expect some punishment for our waywardness. I don't think Ransom's position can be reduced to silliness, Sophia. However, over and beyond the problem of various interpretations of God's teachings, isn't it also a possibility that God would have given us reason, so that with its natural light we could discern something, although perhaps not perfectly, about the best way for humans to lead their lives? If that is not so, what is the point of having reason in the first place? Even if someone doesn't believe in God, he still has reason. Perhaps this is the way the believer can show how God expects even atheists and agnostics to be good.

RANSOM: We have reason because we are cast in the image of God.

BOB: And it may be that by exercising our own independent reason, without a direct reference to religious faith, one may try to understand the nature of our moral experience. Why would God see this as an offense? Couldn't he have given us reason precisely for this purpose? Perhaps in general this is God's will! That we rely on our own judgment.

RANSOM: But why would God have bothered to give us the revelation if we can figure it out on our own?

BOB: Perhaps revelation was required to overcome the laziness and the limitations of human reason. In other words, one might argue that it was provided not because reason is altogether inadequate, just incomplete.

SOPHIA: How would that work?

BOB: Maybe reason could give us a number of important moral principles, but sometimes in specific moral situations God could give us guidance if they appear to conflict.

RANSOM: I still don't buy it. Doesn't it all come down to a matter of determining what God wants for our lives? That's what I've been taught. And religious sources are the only way to find that out, through prayer, reading the Bible, and consulting with other people of God. As I see it, we should live by one principle: What is right is what God wills in our life. What is wrong is what God forbids. God's commands are what makes something right for me.

PETER: Very good. You've stated the principle clearly. It is really a radical attempt to define moral rightness, and it has been maintained by some famous theologians, such as William of Ockham and Emil Brunner.

SARAH: Impressive, Ransom. Fast company.

PETER: Unfortunately, it leads to some very difficult implications. The arguments against this theory, sometimes called the Divine Command Theory, are at least as old as Plato's writings. The standard response appears in one ·of Plato's dialogues, the *Euthyphro.*

RANSOM: Go ahead, Professor. What implications?

PETER: Well, let me put it to you in the form of a question, a very famous question asked by Socrates. You say that we know what actions are right because they are commanded by God. But are they right because God commands them, or does God command them because they are right?

BOB: Ah, I remember.

RANSOM: I don't get it. Say it again.

PETER: All right. Let me put it this way: Is it just the fact that God commands something that makes it right, that is, God's commanding something *causes* it to be right, or does God command it because he knows it's right in the first place?

RANSOM: Why do I have to choose? He knows what is right, and his commands make something right.

PETER: I don't think that you can have it both ways. At least you can't according to your Divine Command Theory. You say something is right *because* God commands it, don't you?

RANSOM: I guess so.

PETER: That's what your theory is. Now, what I want you to do is consider the implications of this position, and then consider the implications of the further question: Why do you suppose that God commands as he does?

RANSOM: All right.

PETER: Suppose that what is right or wrong is simply what God commands or forbids. For example, murder is wrong just because

God says so. Or, take another example, it's morally wrong to abuse children. Suppose we wake up tomorrow and God commands us to devote our day to rape, murder, and child abuse. Then, according to your theory, it would be morally acceptable to rape, murder, and abuse children. According to your view, we would have to accept this rather startling change of moral truth.

RANSOM: That's absurd. God would never do this. He would never change his mind like that. God is perfect. God is morally perfect, all-loving, and all-good.

PETER: But, you see, that is precisely the problem with your position. God cannot be perfect if he makes arbitrary decisions, and that is in fact what he does if moral values are only what they are because of his choice.

RANSOM: But I'm not saying that God makes arbitrary decisions. He's perfect. He always chooses the best decision.

PETER: How do you know they're the best? What does "best" mean here? It must mean that his decisions are *morally best,* but how can you know that? It is at least conceivable that God is all-powerful but he's *not* all-good. To say that he *is* all-good you must have a standard of goodness to make that judgment. But that is precisely what is lacking in your original definition. You say that *whatever* God wills is right or good. But you have to say that God is all-good to avoid the problem of arbitrariness and that means you must have a preexisting moral standard in order to judge that God isn't arbitrary or capricious or evil. Your God isn't arbitrary, is he?

RANSOM: No; he's all-good.

PETER: According to your definition, what would it mean to say that God is good? You define moral terms strictly in relation to God's commands. Right action or good conduct is what God commands. So what would it mean to say that God is good?

SOPHIA: It could only mean that God is commanded by God.

PETER: And that tells us nothing about God's moral nature. Supposedly, God cares for us deeply. He loves us; he's concerned for us. The Divine Command Theory empties the notion of God's goodness of any meaningful moral content.

BOB: So a being could be called "God" if he is very powerful, but he would be unworthy of worship unless we judged that his commandments were morally acceptable.

SOPHIA: For that, we need a moral standard other than a simple appeal to what "God" commands.

PETER: Yes. Another way to look at this is to say that there is an incompatibility between saying that God is "perfect" and saying that moral values are purely determined by God's commands. For if God's commands are not arbitrary, then they are based on good reasons. Consider the implications of our second question. Just ask yourself, *why* does God command as he does?

RANSOM: I, for one, have no idea.

PETER: Of course you do. As a Christian, you believe that God has a certain nature and we can know something about that nature, even if we can't know it perfectly; God is not an irrational, gratuitous being. If God's commands are not purely arbitrary, then they are based on good reasons. If that is the case, God has a reason for his moral commands. Accordingly, if murder is wrong, it is willed by God, not because he simply capriciously chooses it to be wrong, but because he sees clearly the *reason* it is wrong. Hence, if that is the case, you must give up your original position—that an action is right just because God commands it—and you must embrace the opposite position—that God commands actions because they are right. Because he knows they are objectively preferable.

SARAH: Whew! That's heavy.

RANSOM: Okay, I see what you're getting at. Suppose I grant your argument about God's commands. But what difference does it make? All you've succeeded in doing, without realizing it, is to defend my general point that it is from God that we get our moral commands, and those commands are guaranteed by God's perfect knowledge.

BOB: Good point, Ransom! I like that.

PETER: It's certainly true that a person of faith can take comfort in that divine guarantee, although even on this point I think questions of interpretation and application might still arise. But I think that you're mistaken in supposing that, because God's commands are not arbitrary, your position—that religious morals alone can address issues about right and wrong—is vindicated. On the contrary, I see that argument—that God's judgments are not arbitrary—as establishing a place for ethics as an independent or autonomous discipline, a vital discipline, I might add, not just an expression of secular humanism.

BOB: And you're going to show us why.

PETER: Quite simply, if God commands actions *because* they're right, then they're really right. And they're right whether, in fact, God commands them or not.

SOPHIA: I see! That means they're right whether or not we happen to think that God is around to approve of them, or command them to his children. It makes God quite irrelevant, don't you think?

PETER: *If* we can understand what God understands. If God sees the reasons for his moral commands, then such reasons are independent of and logically prior to God's will. And if God understands the reasons for his commands as objective and independent truths—and he must if reasons are taken as *justifications,* not rationalizations—then perhaps other rational beings, that is, persons, can see them also. Perhaps human intellects cannot know them as profoundly as God could, whatever that might mean, but it appears that in principle human knowers, too, can know something about the first principles or ultimate reasons of moral life.

BOB: I find this very paradoxical. It's as if our commitment to God as rational and good commits us to the realization that God is superfluous in ethical matters. If there are things that are really right or wrong, objectively, then they are right or wrong whether or not there happens to be a God. Is that what you're saying? I'm not sure I can go along with that.

SOPHIA: Look at it this way. We really think that murder is wrong because life is valuable, and we think that rape is morally vicious because you can't violate or use a person like that. I think that all Peter is saying is that those actions are really morally wrong, whether or not there happens to be a God. Human beings can suffer and it's wrong to make them suffer for no reason. And whether you're a theist or an atheist, that's the moral bottom line.

RANSOM: But my question is this: If there's no God, why be moral at all? Why not just rob and murder and rape, at will? You say it doesn't matter whether there's a God. Yes! Yes! It matters. What kind of world would this be without God?

SOPHIA: I don't want to be too unkind Ransom, since I know how much God means to so many people, but I also know how much misery and cruelty people have inflicted on others for sup-posedly religious reasons. I sometimes wonder whether it wouldn't be better if we all just bracketed the question of God, lived our lives as best we could, and then, if it turned out that there is some kind of personal, ultimate being that some believe in, I suspect things wouldn't go too badly for us.

BOB: You haven't answered Ransom's question. If there is no God, why be moral at all? Why not just do your own thing?

SOPHIA: Well, it's clear to me that *believing* in God doesn't al-ways make people do the right thing or be a good person. That's certainly part of the issue. And as I've said before, there are ob-viously nonbelievers who are moral people. I don't see any neces-sary relationship between belief in God and being motivated to do the morally right thing.

RANSOM: But why would a person try to do the right thing if there's no God?

PETER: Two points are important here. First, you talk as if the reason for being moral is fear of punishment or hope of reward.

Those are self-interested reasons, not moral reasons. So it's interesting that you seem to think that the only "reason" to be moral is to cover your proverbial backside. This leads me to my second point. Your question, "Why do the right thing?," is an important one. Perhaps we could talk about it at length later. But one obvious answer that appears at least as plausible as your religious one is simply: Because the action in question is right. After all, to say an action is morally right, that it is, for example, right to help others in distress or to keep your word, is to say that often people are motivated to do the right thing simply because they judge the action as morally right. Do you find that answer uninformative? I could say more, but that might lead us to an extended discussion.

RANSOM: Let me think about it. I think I've had enough philosophy for one evening.

SARAH: Come on, Ransom. You sound a little down. You've been a good sport.

BOB: Your challenge made us think. I have one more thought before we hit our sleeping bags. I am sympathetic to Peter's attempt to show that ethics and religious morals aren't necessarily incompatible and that there is probably a large area of agreement between the two. But I'm bothered by the one extreme conclusion, especially as Sophia puts it. Somehow I can't buy the notion that the existence of God is completely irrelevant for all cases of ethical reflection. Think about this. If God exists, he is the creator of everything, as I believe. If this is true, then everything is his and we owe him everything. If he is our father, and creation is his, then that matters, ethically. Doesn't it? Wouldn't that make a difference?

PETER: How?

BOB: Well, we should worship him, for example.

PETER: Is there a *moral* obligation to worship, such that, if God does exist and a person doesn't believe it, he would somehow wrong God by not worshipping? Would it be a failure to fulfill a *moral* obligation?

BOB: I think so. And I think it might have implications in issues like euthanasia and suicide, since, if God is creator, we're his property and we don't have the right to use his property in ways he doesn't approve of.

PETER: Very interesting. *Very* interesting. Bob, have you ever thought of giving up your business and going into philosophy full-time?

BOB: I couldn't afford it. How would you respond, Peter?

PETER: It strikes me that the whole notion of the world as property, and God having property rights, is suspicious. We could, for example, see the world and our lives on the analogy of a gift, and then I think it would be more difficult to sustain your conclusions about special obligations arising *if* God does exist. I shall have to think hard about that. More tomorrow?

BOB: Of course. Sophia?

SOPHIA: I'm game. We'll get the others involved, too. Sleep tight, Ransom. Say some prayers for me!

What Thinkers Have Said

Euthyphro: Yes, I should say that what all the gods love is pious and holy, and the opposite which they all hate, impious.

Plato, *Euthyphro*

Rather, in the Christian view, that alone is "good" which is free from all caprice, which takes place in unconditional obedience. There is no Good save obedient behavior, save the obedient will. But this obedience is rendered not to a law or a principle which can be known beforehand, but only to the free, sovereign will of God. The Good consists in always doing what God wills at any particular moment.

Emil Brunner, *The Divine Imperative*

The Good is simply what God wills that we should do, not that which we would do on the basis of a principle of love. God wills to do something quite definite and particular through us, here and now, something which no other person could do at any other time.

Emil Brunner, *The Divine Imperative*

The Hebrew-Christian ethical perspective also challenges the many species of humanistic ethics so influential in the Western world today. Biblical ethics discredits an autonomous morality. It gives theonomous ethics its classic form—the identification of the moral law with the Divine will. In Hebrew-Christian revelation, distinctions in ethics reduce to what is good or what is pleasing, and to what is wicked or displeasing to the Creator-God alone. . . .

C. F. Henry, *Christian Personal Ethics*

The question what makes an act a duty has been answered ambiguously throughout the whole history of ethics. The view that finds in consequences or good results the obligatory basis of our actions, and conceives the ethical act merely as instrumentally good is inadequate. The view that regards an action itself as intrinsically good with total indifference to its consequences, and derives goodness from obligation, is equally inadequate. Both views fail to grasp the fact that obligation and virtue, goodness and happiness, find their common ground in the Divine will.

C. F. Henry, *Christian Personal Ethics*

Now, what I have been arguing for is the idea that, if certain theological beliefs (that God created the universe but allows man to appropriate the property in it subject to certain restrictions and requirements that he lays down) are true, then men will have rights of stewardship, and not property rights, over the property that they possess. And if this is so, then there will be moral truths (about restrictions and requirements that property-possessors must follow) that might not be true if these theological beliefs were false. So we have here a set of moral claims whose truth or falsehood might depend upon the truth or falsehood of certain theological claims.

Baruch A. Brody, "Morality and Religion Reconsidered"

Key Terms and Concepts

humanism	theology
religion	divine command theory of morality
theism	the *euthyphro* question
natural vs. supernatural	problem of arbitrariness
religious morals	justification vs. rationalization
sin	moral motivation
autonomy of ethics	"right" and "ought"
revelation	obligations to god
philosophy	

Questions

1. In spite of Peter's arguments, are you skeptical about the supposed compatibility between ethics and religious morals?

2. Could it possibly be dangerous to rely on "revelation" as the basis for moral values? Give an example and explain.

3. Reflect on your own motivation to act morally. What is the relation between religious conviction (or lack of conviction) and moral action in your own life? What does Sophia say about the need for religious motivation in moral action?

4. Explain Peter's arguments against the view that what is right or good is simply a function of what God commands.

5. Summarize Peter's position concerning the "autonomy" of ethics.

6. Describe a situation in which religious values could override moral values.

7. Consider Bob's final point about whether the existence of God is completely irrelevant for ethical reflection. How might the discussion continue between Bob and Peter?

Suggested Readings

Brody, Baruch, "Morality and Religion Reconsidered," in *Readings in the Philosophy of Religion: An Analytic Approach*, ed. by Brody, Prentice Hall, Inc., 1974.

Brunner, Heinrich Emil, *The Divine Imperative*, trans. by Olive Wyon, The Westminster Press, 1947.

Helm, Paul, ed., *The Divine Command Theory of Ethics*, Oxford University Press, 1979. An excellent collection of contemporary articles.

Henry, Carl F. H., *Christian Personal Ethics*, Eerdmans, 1957.

Nielsen, Kai, *Ethics without God*, Prometheus Books, 1973. A defense of the superiority of a secular approach to ethics.

Plato, *Euthyphro*, in *The Trial and Death of Socrates*, trans. by G. M. A. Grube, Hackett Publishing Co., 1975. Socrates engages a "fundamentalist" in a trenchant and entertaining criticism of the divine command theory.

Rachels, James, *The Elements of Moral Philosophy*, ch. 4., Random House, 1986. Summarizes the classic criticism in a clear and accessible manner.

Williams, Bernard, *Morality: An Introduction to Ethics*, Harper Torchbooks, 1972. Contains an interesting brief discussion of "God, Morality, and Prudence."

Dialogue Three:
Ethics and Relativism

Reflecting further on the last discussion, Ransom argues again that philosophical ethics, as a discipline autonomous from religion, is unsatisfactory. He argues that, since even the philosopher's thoughts and beliefs are mainly limited to and shaped by his own culture, philosophical ethics will be relative to time and place. Peter argues that it is not obvious that morality differs from culture to culture, and even if there is some cross-cultural moral disagreement, it doesn't follow that morality is simply defined in terms of cultural approval. Finally, relativism is incompatible with many of our most cherished beliefs about morality. These beliefs suggest that autonomous ethical thinking involves appeals to universal standards.

ROSE: Ransom, you look tired today.

RANSOM: I am. I had trouble falling to sleep. My mind kept racing after we stopped talking last night.

SOPHIA: A little tired from the hike, too?

RANSOM: No, not an old vet of the woods like me.

SOPHIA: I bet I know what it was. You kept thinking of all those brilliant comebacks that you couldn't think of at the time, right? Ransom, the philosopher!

RANSOM: Gimme a break, Sophia. You know, I *might* just have something original to offer. As it so happens, I had an insight last night, and I kept tossing and turning and I couldn't get my mind to quit.

SARAH: Go ahead, Albert, let's hear this piece of genius.

RANSOM: Well, there I was, lying under the stars, marveling at God's wonders, trying to shut my mind down so I could fall asleep. And then it occurred to me. A really good idea flashed through my mind. Better than any when I took my philosophy class at school.

SARAH: You mean you had an idea in your class? I never had a clue when I took my philosophy class.

RANSOM: I kept thinking about it all night. I never could fall into a really deep sleep.

BOB: Tell us about it. You *know* you have a captive philosophical audience, at least sitting in my spot!

RANSOM: Okay. Here it is. I think it's a good reply to the kind of secular humanism that you all were defending last night.

SOPHIA: Please! There goes that ugly phrase again, "secular humanism." Peter, do you want to slap his knuckles with a ruler?

BOB: How about "philosophical ethics," rather than "secular humanism"? I wasn't defending what the fundamentalists call secular humanism. I could see, however, why we need to defend the value of philosophical ethics.

RANSOM: All right. I stand corrected. Anyway, my argument is this. Peter said yesterday that religious revelation isn't the standard for philosophical ethics. Right?

PETER: Yes. But remember my caution that the ethician need not be actually opposed to religion.

RANSOM: I remember. But one reason that revelation is difficult to establish as a standard, you said, is because there are so many so-called "revelations," each claiming to be the *one* revealed word of God. Right so far?

PETER: Correct. Go on.

RANSOM: Well, I got to thinking. Isn't the same true when we think about values alone, apart from religion? I mean, Sophia here pretty much dismissed my appeal to Christianity as the one true standard for religion, because people in other cultures interpret revelation differently. Well, I'm saying that the same kind of criticism applies to secular . . . sorry, I mean *philosophical* thinking about values. Unless you philosophers are going to patently ignore the facts, cultures disagree about moral values even more than they disagree about religion.

SARAH: Ransom, I think you're on to something here.

SOPHIA: I'm not sure where you're going with this supposed "insight." So cultures might disagree about morality. So what?

RANSOM: Look. What I mean is just this: Peter says that ethics tries to tell us about what is right and wrong about human behavior. You wouldn't let me appeal to Christianity because it's not common to all cultures, and even within Christianity there's disagreement. But how can philosophy tell us what is right and wrong when societies differ so radically about moral values?

SARAH: I see where you're coming from. Societies disagree about morals. You're saying that philosophy can't tell you what *the* right thing is, everywhere.

RANSOM: But I'm not a relativist.

SARAH: You just said you were.

RANSOM: If philosophers want to look for *the* correct standards to evaluate moral conduct, then they have to realize that moral values vary, just like religious beliefs. But I believe in absolutes. I believe that God commands his creatures everywhere, and what he says is absolute. Why should I accept Peter's arguments that ethics can find universal standards of morality? How can *human* judgments, limited in terms of place, form a "science" called ethics when people the world over differ so much in their moral beliefs?

SARAH: Very interesting.

RANSOM: In other words, if a philosopher wants to say what is *really* right and wrong, everywhere, then he has to be an absolutist. But how can you have absolutism if you rule out an appeal to God's commands? All you're left with is society to tell you what's right and wrong, and societies disagree about morality.

PETER: That's an interesting argument, and logically quite provocative. Ransom, you seem to think that philosophical ethics is committed to some kind of absolutism in ethics, since it wants to find valid standards for judging human conduct and character, everywhere, across cultures. But you also argue that the only way to ground that absolutism is by an appeal to what might be called *transcendental* moral standards instead of social standards, since societies disagree about morality and that inevitably leads to relativism. So the logically unhappy result of secular, philosophical, ethics is the contradictory desire for absolute standards while ruling out the necessary condition for such standards.

SARAH: Is that what he said? I don't see the big deal. Isn't it obvious that cultures disagree about morals? If you're saying that ethics looks for absolutes, then I really question that. I guess I'm a relativist. Cultures have their own values. What right do we have prying into other societies' ways of life?

PETER: What Ransom has done here is to bring up the old problem of cultural relativism, which is, generally speaking, the view that there is no moral belief common to all cultures or societies. But over and beyond this rather general description, the expression "cultural relativism" is subject to a number of different interpretations. As a matter of fact, people seem to mean different things by the expression. Let's attempt to clarify it.

SARAH: It's pretty clear to me. Moral beliefs differ among societies. People believe different things. Right?

PETER: Is that it, Ransom? If that's your view, then it appears to be uncontroversially true, at least in *some* sense.

RANSOM: That's part of it. But I'm saying something stronger than that. I'm more interested in what results from the fact that cultures disagree about their moral beliefs, and all you have is *human* thinking to decide what's right and wrong.

PETER: I gathered as much from what you've said thus far. Tell me if I correctly represent your position. You explain cultural relativism as an assertion of fact, if I can speak philosophically. In other words, you say you are just *describing* the fact that people in different cultures have different moral beliefs. But you also think this leads to a *normative* conclusion: namely, that *because* moral beliefs vary so widely (that's your premise), *therefore*, negatively, one can never argue for a judgment of right or wrong that is universal. That is, there aren't any moral standards that would be valid and binding for all people, regardless of geography and history. How would we put the normative conclusion positively? If moral standards aren't universal or "absolute," they're . . . ?

SARAH: Relative.

PETER: Relative to what?

SARAH: To society.

PETER: So what *is* right, according to relativism? What is the positive normative thesis?

BOB: I suppose it's that whatever is right is what a society happens to hold as right at some time and place in history.

RANSOM: That's what I think follows. That's exactly what I have in mind, if I remember what you said the word "normative" means. I don't see how ethics can find anything universally applicable to all people since as human beings we're all part of a culture, and the same goes for our moral beliefs. Who's to say what is universally right?

PETER: Besides God?

RANSOM: If we're culturally limited, our values are culturally limited as well. Without what you're calling a *transcendent* source, our moral values would just come from cultural or social sources. And that means that ethics is worthless. If ethics can't say something valid for all people, what's the point? It makes it a pseudoscience. How can laws of ethics be binding when there's no agreement among the people of the world as to what they are? Ethics drowns in the swamp called "cultural relativism," which brings us back to where we started yesterday: I mean, that a purely human ethics is a sham. Without God, there's no real ethics, just sinful and proud humans with their social mores.

SOPHIA: But don't forget *your* big problem, Ransom. Your religious moral beliefs might just be how *your* culture interprets the supposed word of God. If your argument is right, if *mere* human judgment is all we have and it's as fallible as you say, then you better be a relativist, or at least not be intolerant of other religious moral views that differ radically from yours.

BOB: Sophia, you did make a lot out of the fact that people have differing interpretations of God's revelation.

SOPHIA: But I agree with Peter. I have more faith in human reason to find the truth, to make sound judgments about how we ought to live and how we ought to treat people. I heard you saying the same things, but giving them a religious slant. I think that reason is more than just a slave to the cultural and social factors that influence us. We can think! That's our genius.

BOB: I believe God gave us the power to use our reason, in morality as well as elsewhere.

SOPHIA: But I admit he's brought up a tough criticism. On the face of it, what he says seems hard to discount. Cultural differences obviously count for a lot in our thinking about values. I realize that. How could any philosopher ever change that? But I think there's a difference between cultures *causing* beliefs and cultures *influencing* us.

SARAH: Philosophers can't change the fact that we're all different. You know, variety is the spice of life.

MARK: But *is* there as much difference as we think? Think of all the talk these days about human rights. Aren't these rights for *everyone*, everywhere? Like our Bill of Rights?

BOB: As Ransom said, you can't deny the facts. That cultures *do* differ in their moral beliefs is as obvious as night and day. Surely most of you have read or heard about the studies of anthropologists.

RANSOM: That's it! Hey, even I've read *National Geographic*. It's striking. As we were hiking today, I was trying to think of as many examples as I could to support my case, examples of what Peter has called "cultural relativism." I jotted some of them down.

SOPHIA: Did you also jot down examples of what happened to some cultures when good Christian missionaries went to places and decided that "God" didn't like what these people were doing?

ROSE: Sophia, let Ransom go on.

RANSOM: For example, I've heard that some societies actually eat their dead rather than bury or burn them. We would call such a practice barbaric. But no doubt they would regard our practice of burial or cremation as barbaric.

PETER: I believe Herodotus' *History* describes that. And what about cannibals?

SOPHIA: But is it really appropriate to stack the deck in Ransom's favor with examples like these? It's much easier to point out differences if you refer only to the customs of primitive people.

PETER: But, if I may speak on Ransom's behalf for a moment, one must be careful about remarks like that, Sophia. The argument that Ransom is offering is challenging the very assumption that one can ever judge people to be inferior or superior to others. Hence, relativism rules out ever calling some cultures "primitive." It's a value-laden term.

RANSOM: Remember, I'm saying that Christian faith is our only true refuge as far as morality goes, so from the standpoint of religion one *can* judge one society superior to another. Missionaries of God had an obligation to lovingly teach primitive people about God's way.

SOPHIA: Like the horrible, sinful practice of females walking around with their breasts uncovered. How shameful!

BOB: Anyway, cannibalism seems to support cultural relativism. In some cultures, it has been quite the moral fashion. Cannibals seem to be downright self-righteous about it. They probably think they're superior to other societies precisely because of it!

RANSOM: What about the stories you hear about Eskimos? They kill the members of the tribe who are too old and feeble to survive the harsh winters as the tribe migrates.

SARAH: We'd call that murder.

MARK: And take them to court!

SARAH: We send our old folks to nursing homes. Maybe the Eskimos have a better idea about how to treat their old people.

PETER: What about homosexuality and prostitution? In our culture, these are generally considered unacceptable, but in others they are looked upon as more a matter of taste than of morality. I'm sure some people in our culture would be shocked by some things in Plato's *Symposium*, for example.

MARK: This even applies to beliefs we hold most dear. In Western cultures, we believe that private property is an inalienable right. In some societies, it's considered the root of all evil.

SOPHIA: What about our attitudes to other creatures of the earth? Some cultures think that animals may be treated in any way people choose. Even some "Christians" believe it. Some groups don't care about cruelty to animals. But many people, even most, in the Western world at least, would consider wanton cruelty to animals morally repulsive.

PETER: I think that it would be safe to say that some of the most atrocious behaviors—at least, things that *we* consider atrocious—have at some time in some society had their fashion, whereas behaviors that we would consider perfectly acceptable have been condemned in some societies and still are. Consider the Mormons' taste for polygamy, and incest among the Egyptians. Such practices have not only been accepted; they've sometimes been vigorously promoted! On the other hand, activities seemingly as innocent as dancing and charging interest for loans have been condemned in some places.

SARAH: So how can there be universal standards for right and wrong? What's right in one place isn't right in others. We're talking about different customs, that's all.

PETER: So moral standards are simply customs that happen to be accepted or approved at particular times in the histories of cultures?

BOB: So we throw ethics out the window? I don't believe that.

PETER: I don't either.

SARAH: You wouldn't, Peter. You'd be out of a job.

PETER: It might appear that the cultural relativist has made an impressive case, and I must admit that the ordinary person, and I don't mean that in a derogatory way, is usually sympathetic to this line of reasoning. But philosophers have seldom been much impressed by such arguments.

SARAH: But you've already admitted that it's a fact that cultures have different moral beliefs. It sounds to me like the relativist's case is airtight. No doubt there's a lot of disagreement.

PETER: Let's be careful here. The relativist says that the crucial issue is the very *fact* of moral disagreement among cultures. But I want to probe four different questions. First, what is the *level* of this disagreement? Might it be, at least in some cases, more superficial than real? Second, even if there is real disagreement, how *extensive* is it? In other words, the emphasis on disagreement might be misleading if it covers up significant agreement among cultures about morally significant values. Third, what *follows* from whatever disagreement *is* the case, if there are disagreements? In other words, what is the relevance of disagreement in relation to the possibility of philosophical ethics. Finally, what should be our own *attitude* toward real moral differences? Notice we haven't even mentioned this, but the relativist recommends tolerance.

BOB: You have the floor.

PETER: I don't want the floor. I want you people to help me think through these things. Suppose we take an example of the disagreement just between us, then ask why we have the disagreement. Let me suggest the issue of abortion. I suspect there is disagreement among us about the moral permissibility of abortion. Why do we disagree?

ANTHONY: May I step in? I've thought some about this, as most of us probably have. I see one side insisting the fetus is human, so you can't kill it. I see the other side realizing there are many other important factors to be considered when the decision is made, and the decision is best made privately, by the female.

SOPHIA: There's something else here. I simply find the rhetoric about "person-at-the-moment-of-conception" to be unconvincing. One cell isn't a human person, or a child, or a baby, however the prolifers talk.

BOB: But it is human; you can't deny that fact.

SOPHIA: The fact I deny is that a one-celled member of the human species is what we call a person.

PETER: Do you disagree about whether it's wrong to kill innocent "persons"?

SOPHIA: Of course not.

PETER: So this disagreement is not moral at all. You disagree about a question of fact: Is the fetus a human person? You disagree about whether the concept of personhood includes a fetus. Extend this to the supposed fact of cultural disagreement. Don't just accept the disagreement as obvious. Ask *why* there is disagreement. Is the disagreement really a *moral* one at all?

BOB: You're suggesting that most cultural disagreements aren't *moral* disagreements at all?

PETER: I hesitate to say "most," but when you identify a case of supposed moral disagreement, you have to ask whether it is *really*, or only *apparently*, a case of moral disagreement. It often happens that the disagreement is not about morality at all. It's often about differing belief systems, about scientific judgments or religious beliefs, that is, about *nonmoral* matters. Take the case of cannibals. Ransom, do you recall in your anthropological studies why the practice occurs? What do they believe?

RANSOM: Something like the fact that if they eat their enemies, they'll acquire their positive qualities. I think that's what we read.

SOPHIA: So it's really because of their weird nonmoral beliefs that their moral habits, or what we would call their moral habits, become what they are. We don't share their religious beliefs, and those are the basis for their moral beliefs. If we did, we might not consider cannibalism morally offensive at all. [Grinning.] And, by the way, some people in our own culture don't seem to mind eating flesh and drinking blood. Know what they are called? Bob, you should know.

BOB: No.

SOPHIA: Catholics!

ROSE: Another cheap shot, dear.

BOB: Should I explain the metaphysical background of transubstantiation in the philosophy of Aristotle and Aquinas?

SOPHIA: That's precisely the point, isn't it? The way our metaphysical or religious beliefs affect actions that then get conceived differently and judged morally.

PETER: And this suggests that much of what passes for moral disagreement, about which the relativist makes so much, may not be about differences of value at all. Therefore, we don't necessarily have to accept what first appears as obviously true, that cultures differ in their moral beliefs.

RANSOM: But what about cases where it must be about moral values? For example, certain South Sea islanders are expected to put their parents to death at middle age. Not only do these people not consider this practice murder, the tribe positively expects it. If a son or daughter doesn't kill his or her parents, then it's wrong. They're considered a bad child. We'd consider that murder; they consider it their highest duty. That's a moral conflict, isn't it?

BOB: I'd guess the reply would be much the same. We need to ask *why* they do this. We need to know *what* they think about when killing a parent.

PETER: As I understand it, these islanders don't kill their parents out of a desire to murder; they feel obligated to do so for religious reasons. As I recall, these people believe that one must die in relatively good health in order to fend for oneself in the afterlife. It is out of love and honor for one's parents that the child must kill them. Do *we* hold that one must love and honor one's parents and do what is best for them?

SOPHIA: Of course we do. Now I see what you're getting at by asking about the *level* of disagreement. We might treat our parents differently, but it's because of different belief systems. Basically, or at a deeper level, we agree about how to treat our parents morally.

PETER: Right. As it turns out, there may be more agreement about *values* than meets the eye. This example shows that, while there is disagreement on one level between islanders and our culture, on a deeper level there appears to be no disagreement at all. There is a moral judgment that both cultures accept.

SOPHIA: That we should love and honor our parents.

PETER: Exactly. It may be that relativism only occurs with regard to superficial or secondary moral beliefs or factual beliefs, whereas there is agreement with reference to deeper or primary or ultimate beliefs.

BOB: I see what you're saying: Societies derive a variety of rules, practices, and applications from their most basic or cherished moral beliefs, and the differences between cultures may be only in these derivations or applications rather than in the most basic moral values themselves.

PETER: I can't speak for all anthropologists, but influential anthropologists like Sumner and Ruth Benedict and even Westermarck seem not to have been sensitive to this crucial distinction. In the islanders example, the basic principle that people should love and honor their parents gets applied in one way in their culture, another in ours. It's a difference in applications because of different nonmoral beliefs, not different moral beliefs.

RANSOM: But how can you be so sure that there *is* always a so-called "basic belief" that is held in common?

PETER: You probably can't.in every case. But that is a problem for the relativist, isn't it? Once we've made this crucial distinction, we realize that the relativist must prove that there never *are* such basic beliefs common to all peoples in order to justify his position. Isn't the burden of proof on the relativist, to show not only that societies disagree with regard to their derivative or less basic value beliefs, but also with regard to their most basic or ultimate ones as well? That is difficult to prove, and as far as I know, no anthropologist has proved this.

BOB: I'm not sure how the relativist could prove that. How could he ever convince us that there is no basic moral belief shared by all societies? That's what he holds, isn't it?

PETER: If he's a careful relativist, he might hold that there is at least *some* very basic disagreement, not that there is no agreement at all. But as soon as he makes even this distinction, there's reason to think that, even if he's right about this weaker claim, it's far less devastating than one might think. If there's only *some* disagreement, there might be considerable agreement, and that would be the basis for common modes of moral reasoning and shared ways to resolve moral conflicts.

SARAH: But I think that you all have made relativism look weak because of the kinds of examples you've focused on. Think about this. You have two societies that obviously disagree about moral values, and each is right! It happens doesn't it? What's right, here, isn't right somewhere else. What if two societies differ about . . . uh . . .

MARK: How about property?

SARAH: Okay. Suppose it's really true that for us it's right to own private property, but it's not right for some other culture. Isn't that evidence for relativism?

PETER: Even if we grant your argument about property, it doesn't prove relativism. You're just talking about commonsense differences in light of the fact that situations differ. For example, we say it's wrong to cut someone with a knife when we are robbing him in a dark alley, but we don't say it's wrong for a surgeon to do the same thing in the operating room. Why? Does that make us relativists?

SOPHIA: Of course not. The situations are different, so we have to judge the actions differently.

SARAH: But if something is *really* right, here, and *really* wrong, somewhere else? What about that?

SOPHIA: You can judge the differences according to the same principle. You shouldn't harm another needlessly. Therefore, it's wrong to stab someone in a robbery, but it's not wrong for a surgeon to perform an operation.

PETER: And this appeal to a common standard is just what the relativist forbids, because she denies that there are such common principles or standards. So differences don't prove relativism, even if they do show that an action can be right and wrong at different times in different places, depending on changed needs and applications. As one philosopher put it, one may as well talk about gravitational relativism because a stone falls to the ground and a balloon rises, when, in fact, they are different manifestations of one and the same principle, or law, of gravitation.

RANSOM: But what is the common principle in the hypothetical .case about private property?

PETER: Perhaps it's something as simple as the truth that a society should promote only those practices that insure it's overall well-being.

ANTHONY: So if private property is the right practice in tribe "x" but the wrong one in tribe "y" that doesn't prove relativism, since the difference may be that private property does make "x" happier and doesn't make "y" happier, because of different circumstances.

PETER: The difference may be the result of two different, but appropriate, applications of the principle that a society should, given its geographical and historical circumstances, do whatever makes its people happiest. The two would have different, but sensible, derivations of the same basic and *shared* moral value.

SOPHIA: Besides, I suspect all the emphasis on disagreements and differences may be misleading. I know there are probably real differences, and we now know how to analyze them. But what about the things we share in common with all cultures? Isn't it obvious that some basic values have to be pretty much the same in all societies if we are going to live together? We couldn't have society or social living without certain agreements.

BOB: That crossed my mind earlier. Obviously, every society has to care for the nurturing of babies, otherwise they'd never grow up to be adults; eventually, the result would be no society.

PETER: Even the most stubborn relativist would have to admit that. But there seems to be the same need for the value of truth telling in a society as well. Imagine a social group that doesn't value truth telling or has no moral sanctions against deception.

ANTHONY: How could we talk to each other?

PETER: In order for social interactions to generate social well-being, people have to assume that when serious speech is going on, people are being honest; that is to say, their words (and even their behavior, for that matter) must accurately represent their thoughts. If we couldn't presume this, in a general way, society would fall into chaos. And I know of one famous anthropologist who makes these points straightforwardly. In all cultures, there are notions of unjustified killing, obligations between parents and children, and duties involving contractual arrangements or promises.

SOPHIA: So morality could *be* inherently social, not transcendentally grounded, as Ransom wants, and it still could be universal and nonrelative.

PETER: Yes, in the descriptive sense that we have been investigating. But recall my other questions. There might *be* some basic disagreements among cultures, even if it is inevitable that there

probably is a great deal of agreement about basic moral values. I
know of one philosopher who gives as an example our basic attitudes toward animals. It looks like that would be an example of a
nonmoral disagreement because some cultures might view animals
as soulless machines. But he insists that's not what they believe.
Now, let's suppose there is some basic disagreement. What follows
from this? Why is it relevant?

SOPHIA: What do you mean?

PETER: What follows concerning what *is*, in fact, right or wrong?
Is moral rightness "relative" to a culture if there *are* some basic
disagreements about moral values? Recall how the relativist defines
what's right.

BOB: What is right is whatever a culture approves of or whatever
it happens to permit or not prohibit.

PETER: This is a rather subtle point for some people to grasp.
The cultural relativist usually holds two different positions, a descriptive thesis and a normative thesis. (I hope that language is clear
by now.) And he holds that there is a logical relationship between
the two. He offers us an argument. To put it quite simply, it's a
bad argument. It is logically invalid.

BOB: Better go slowly here.

PETER: An argument is merely the attempt to give reasons for
some belief. The relativist holds that what is morally right is what
is approved by a particular group or culture. He defends that normative thesis by giving us a reason or justification for it. That's his
premise that cultures disagree about moral values. He says that,
since there is moral disagreement, then values must be relative; what
is right is defined by social approval. Now, generally, when someone gives an argument he is saying, *if* you accept my premises, you
must accept my conclusion. So the argument is, indeed, a good one
if his premises guarantee his conclusion, and it is a poor one, an
invalid one, if we grant him the truth of his premises but we show
that his conclusion may *not* be the case. In other words, his argument is bad if his premises aren't really adequate to establish his
conclusion.

SARAH: Say again what the premises and the conclusion are.

PETER: The argument is this: Because moral values are thought about so differently, values must be relative. Or, to put it differently, disagreement entails truth relativity. What is morally right must be socially relative because there is disagreement about moral values.

BOB: So ethics, as the search for universal and objective moral standards, would be impossible.

PETER: Yes. Well? Can you see why the argument is invalid?

SARAH: Invalid?

PETER: Why the premises don't guarantee the conclusion?

SARAH: But if you have cultures disagreeing, how *can* there be one right answer?

PETER: All right. Think of this in terms of disagreements between individuals. If individuals disagree about something, does it follow that what is true is relative?

SARAH: It depends on what they disagree about.

PETER: The relativist's argument makes no case for the distinctiveness of moral disagreement. She simply says, if there is disagreement, truth must be relative, or, what is right in our society is different from what is right somewhere else.

BOB: I smell something fishy here. From the mere fact that people disagree about something can we infer that there is no objective truth in the matter? Just because there is disagreement, do we have to conclude that neither party in the dispute is right? I don't think so.

PETER: Can you give me an example?

SOPHIA: This morning Rose and I had a disagreement about the highest peak in Wyoming. She said it was Gannett Peak and I said it wasn't. I knew one of us had to be right. As it turned out, she was. I thought it was Granite Peak, but that's in Montana. We resolved our disagreement.

BOB: So it wasn't true that just because there was disagreement, what was "right" for Sophia wasn't "right" for Rose.

PETER: It's a point that hardly reaches beyond common sense, but it's a very difficult one for some of my students to see. Mere disagreement doesn't entail the relativity of truth. Why? Because one side could be right and the other wrong. For that matter, *agreement* doesn't entail truth. Just because we all agree on something doesn't make it true or right. We could all be participating in a shared mistake. Truth isn't established by consensus, and lack of objective truth isn't proved by disagreement. We have to investigate what the evidence is, what the reasons are for some belief, if we want to find out whether it's true. Likewise, it may be the task of ethics to determine, by reflection on the disagreement, using reason, which party in a disagreement is right. In that way, ethics is not culturally bound, but is, as we said earlier, able to transcend cultural constraints and able to stand as an independent discipline.

SOPHIA: Doesn't the relativist adopt a very unscientific attitude? She seems to think that moral disagreement is just a given fact that we can never rise above. But some cultures may not be as enlightened as others. I'm not being snobbish, either. Maybe *we* need enlightenment from other cultures. But some peoples may be more ignorant than others, and this may influence their level of civilization, their level of moral thinking. We're under no obligation to think that another society has a right to think that the earth is flat. We don't have to withhold judgment about flat-earth believers. The same goes for moral matters, if they believe in some repugnant kind of practice.

SARAH: But in science you can prove what's true. How do you do that for morals?

PETER: That's the big question! It would be naive to believe that moral reasoning or justification is no different from scientific justification. But that is *precisely* why ethics is important, to consider what moral reasoning looks like and not give up the entire project at the outset because someone might reason so badly as to suppose that disagreement means truth is relative. If some people or some culture has some belief, as rational creatures we want to ask *why* they have that belief. And that is a "why" of logic, of justification, not the scientific "why" looking for causal explanations.

BOB: So the point really is that if the argument is bad, we're under no obligation to accept relativism.

PETER: We can say that the central argument for the view that moral rightness is simply a matter of social approval is a bad one. Our criticism doesn't prove that relativism is wrong; it's just that relativism hasn't adequately defended its position. We have no reason, at this time, to believe it. We can, however, offer considerations that, to my mind, tip the scales quite heavily against relativism. Let's suppose that rightness *is* a matter of social approval. Let's see how this view squares with other beliefs we have.

MARK: Such as?

PETER: I've heard some of them mentioned in the course of our conversation. For example, if someone says something patently false, like "the earth is flat," we reject it. Is there anything analogous in morality? That is, just because a culture or social group approves of "x," does that mean that "x" is right?

SOPHIA: It's the same problem we talked about last night with the Divine Command Theory. If a society approves of slavery, or gassing Jews, that doesn't make it right.

PETER: That's the sort of classic counterexample usually offered. Social authority doesn't constitute moral rightness, since a given social group could be disastrously mistaken from the moral point of view, as they often have been.

SOPHIA: If there are moral values that are and ought to be universally accepted, like the fact that you can't enslave other human beings, then some cultures really can be superior or inferior to others.

PETER: And progress? Or decline? Can societies progress, morally?

ANTHONY: Of course. The fact that we abolished slavery means that we have progressed, although we have a long way to go.

PETER: Just ask yourself: If relativism were true, if right was just a matter of social approval, could a society progress? What would be the standard to make such a judgment? If, as a society, we once approved of slavery, and now we don't, could the relativist standard of rightness explain our judgment that we have made moral progress?

BOB: That's very interesting. If we approved of slavery then slavery would have been right, at least according to the relativist.

PETER: So?

BOB: So although we *now* believe slavery was mistaken, we can't use our current standard for judging the past.

PETER: And that's because moral rightness is relative, according to the relativist. So he could only say we've changed our moral views, not that we've progressed. He must say that in the past slavery really *was* right.

SOPHIA: A paradox?

PETER: No. I would say an unacceptable consequence of his doctrine. And what about people who attempt to change the moral status quo? Are they ever morally correct to do so?

ALICE: Like Martin Luther King, Jr.?

SOPHIA: Or Mahatma Gandhi?

PETER: If relativism is true, the moral rebel in a society must necessarily be mistaken, because he attempts to fight what is actually approved in a society, and what is approved must be right. That must mean that if we believe it is sometimes acceptable to overturn the moral status quo, we don't really believe that what is morally right is simply a matter of social approval. Think also about how we make our own moral judgments.

BOB: We try to think about the issues, don't we?

SOPHIA: We examine the arguments and try to find out what the best argument is.

PETER: If normative relativism were correct, how would we attempt to find out what's right?

MARK: Probably by taking a poll.

PETER: Yes, and I can't stress this too much. We just don't decide about moral matters based on what the majority of people happen to think. We have to make our own judgment, based on what we judge to be the best arguments.

ANTHONY: There's something else I find puzzling. We talked a lot about tribes and smaller cultural groups. If group approval is the key to morality, what if I'm in more than one group? What if I'm a member of a tribe in a larger country? What would make something right?

PETER: Many philosophers have also pointed out that difficulty. The whole notion of a social or cultural group as morally sovereign might be practically quite a problem because a person might be, simultaneously, a member of different cultural groups.

SARAH: But if we reject relativism and accept absolutism, that means that we think we know what's right for everyone. Remember, Peter mentioned tolerance. All that stuff about superior and inferior cultures sounds judgmental.

SOPHIA: I meant that the difference between the superior and the inferior is that some cultures, perhaps by being better enlightened in scientific and other nonmoral respects, *might* be more equipped to understand and to appreciate values that others cannot. I also believe that our highly technological and consumer-oriented culture might have a great deal to learn from other less "advanced" cultures. In any case, I don't believe that we have to be tolerant when we see human rights systematically violated in other countries. When we hear that people are tortured somewhere, I don't think our attitude ought to be, "Gee, what's right for them isn't right for us."

PETER: The whole issue of tolerance is a difficult one. I should point out, as most philosophers do, that if the relativist recommends tolerance toward the moral beliefs of all other cultures, she appears to be inconsistent. You can't recommend universal tolerance if you're a relativist. In fact, tolerance appears to be based on the notion that we should respect everyone's moral views, *everywhere*. That looks suspiciously like a universal moral value, doesn't it?

SARAH: So we shouldn't be tolerant?

PETER: I'm not saying that at all. Cultural relativism, in spite of its weaknesses, should be appreciated for pointing out to the philosopher, and others as well, some valuable lessons: for example, that a society should be open-minded before judging other cultures and that a people should be more alive to self-criticism and should be more open to its own moral advancement.

SOPHIA: I believe that's crucial for us, for any society.

PETER: Notice a final startling consequence of relativism. A contemporary philosopher, Mary Midgley, in a marvelous essay, brings this out beautifully. She calls cultural relativism "moral isolationism," and asks us to consider placing a kind of moral barrier between ourselves and other cultures. The relativist usually focuses only on the issue of intolerance, as if the primary judgment involved is always condemnation of other ways of life. But an isolationist moral barrier that insulates us from other cultures also blocks praise, and it blocks the notion that others can judge *us*. It rules out the notion that we might learn about ourselves by comparing *our* moral habits with those of other cultures. And, in fact, this notion of separate, isolated cultures is simply unrealistic, as she says.

RANSOM: So you guys are bound and determined to have your secular humanism.

BOB: Ransom, did you ever stop to think that there might be such a thing as a Christian humanism?

SOPHIA: Or a Jewish humanism? Or an Islamic humanism? Or a Buddhist humanism? Or how about just a "human" humanism, so we treat each other better?

RANSOM: Okay, okay. Maybe we can talk more about this later. I give. At least I can get some sleep if I surrender. Good night, all.

What Thinkers Have Said

For if one were to offer men to choose out of all the customs in the world such as seemed to them the best, they would examine the whole number, and end by preferring their own; so convinced are they that their own usages far surpass those of all others. Unless, therefore, a man was mad, it is not likely that he would make sport of such matter. That people have this feeling about their laws may be seen by very many proofs: among others, by the following. Darius, after he had got the kingdom, called into his presence certain Greeks who were at hand, and asked— "What he should pay them to eat the bodies of their fathers when they died?" To which they answered, that there was no sum that would tempt them to do such a thing. He then sent for certain Indians, of the race called Callatians, men who eat their fathers, and asked them, while the Greeks stood by, and knew by the help of an interpreter all that was said—"What he should give them to burn the bodies of their fathers at their decease?" The Indians exclaimed aloud, and bade him forbear such language. Such is men's wont herein; and Pindar was right in my judgment, when he said, "Law is the king o'er all."

Herodotus, *The Histories*

THE FOLKWAYS ARE "RIGHT." RIGHTS. MORALS. The folkways are the "right" ways to satisfy all interests, because they are traditional, and exist in fact. They extend over the whole of life. There is a right way to catch game, to win a wife, to make one's self appear, to cure disease, to honor ghosts, to treat comrades or strangers, to behave when a child is born, on the warpath, in council, and so on in all cases which can arise. The ways are defined on the negative side, that is, by taboos. The "right" way is the way which the ancestors used and which has been handed down. The tradition is its own warrant. It is not held subject to verification by experience. The notion of right is in the folkways. It is not outside of them, of independent origin, and brought to them to test them. In the folkways, whatever is, is right.

William Graham Sumner, *Folkways*

"Rights" are the rules of mutual give and take in the competition of life which are imposed on comrades in the in-group, in order that the peace may prevail

there which is essential to the group strength. Therefore rights can never be "natural" or "God-given," or absolute in any sense. The morality of a group at a time is the sum of the taboos and prescriptions in the folkways by which right conduct is defined. Therefore morals can never be intuitive. They are historical, institutional, and empirical.

William Graham Sumner, *Folkways*

In fact, the real process in great bodies of men is not one of deduction from any great principle of philosophy or ethics. It is one of minute efforts to live well under existing conditions, which efforts are repeated indefinitely by great numbers, getting strength from habit and from the fellowship of united action. The resultant folkways become coercive. All are forced to conform, and the folkways dominate the societal life. Then they seem true and right, and arise into mores as the norm of welfare. Thence are produced faiths, ideas, doctrines, religions, and philosophies, according to the stage of civilization and the fashions of reflection and generalization.

William Graham Sumner, *Folkways*

It is a point that has been made more often in relation to ethics than in relation to psychiatry. We do not any longer make the mistake of deriving the morality of our own locality and decade directly from the inevitable constitution of human nature. We do not elevate it to the dignity of a first principle. We recognize that morality differs in every society, and is a convenient term for socially approved habits. Mankind has always preferred to say, "It is morally good," rather than "It is habitual," and the fact of this preference is matter enough for a critical science of ethics. But historically the two phrases are synonymous.

Ruth Benedict, "Anthropology and the Abnormal"

To hold that values do not exist because they are relative to time and place, or to deny the psychological validity of differing concepts of reality, is to fall prey to a fallacy that results from a failure to take into account the positive contribution of the relativistic position. For cultural relativism is a philosophy which, in recognizing the values set up by every society to guide its own life, lays stress on the dignity inherent in every body of custom, and on the need for tolerance of conventions though they may differ from one's own. Instead of underscoring differences from absolute norms that, however objectively arrived at, are nonetheless the product of a given time or place, the relativistic point of view brings into relief the validity of every set of norms for the people whose lives are guided by them, and the values these represent.

M. J. Herskovits, *Man and His Works: The Science of Cultural Anthropology*

Key Terms and Concepts

cultural relativism	rights
normative relativism	moral progress
barbarism	moral reform
apparent moral disagreement	method of making moral judgments
real moral disagreement	group approval
nature of disagreement	tolerance
argument	moral isolationism
appeal to counterexample	

Questions

1. Distinguish between cultural relativism as a descriptive thesis and relativism as a normative one (that is, as a definition of what is morally right).

2. Review the four critical questions that Peter asks in response to cultural relativism.

3. Explain why the issue of the level of disagreement among cultures is crucial for evaluating the strength of the relativist's position.

4. Try to list a series of values or moral principles that one might expect to find in all cultures. Explain why each would be important for social life.

5. Explain why the central argument for normative relativism is a bad one.

6. Offer a counterexample to the notion that what is morally right is simply a matter of cultural, social, or group approval.

7. Why does the relativist have a difficult time explaining our commonsense

judgment about the possibility of moral progress and the appropriateness of some acts of moral reform?

8. Why is the relativist inconsistent in recommending tolerance of moral values in every other culture?

9. Are there any positive insights associated with cultural relativism?

10. What seems to be true about moral isolationism? Untrue? Give examples based on our current historical situation.

11. Relativism is sometimes confused with nihilism and moral skepticism. How would you explain the meanings of these three terms?

Suggested Readings

Benedict, Ruth, "Anthropology and the Abnormal," *Journal of General Psychology*, X, 1934.

Brandt, Richard, *Ethical Theory*, Prentice-Hall, 1959. Especially good discussion of descriptive relativism.

Harman, Gilbert, "Moral Relativism Defended," *Philosophical Review*, 84, 1975. A sophisticated contemporary defense of moral relativism.

Herodotus, *History of Herodotus*, trans. by George Rawlinson, Everyman Library, E. P. Dutton and Co., 1910. The source of the famous passage quoted above.

Herskovits, M. J., *Man and His Works: The Science of Cultural Anthropology*, Knopf, 1948.

Midgley, Mary, *Heart and Mind: The Varieties of Moral Experience*, St. Martin's Press, 1981. Her criticisms of "moral isolationism" appear in the chapter "On Trying Out One's New Sword."

Rachels, James, *The Elements of Moral Philosophy*, ch. 2., Random House, 1986. Careful and clear assessment of relativism; gives special attention to problems of validity in the cultural relativist's argument.

Stace, W. T., *The Concept of Morals*, Macmillan, 1937. The book contains a widely anthologized criticism of relativism. Very accessible.

Sumner, William Graham, *Folkways*, Ginn and Co., 1906. The classic presentation of cultural relativism by an anthropologist.

Dialogue Four:
Ethics and Self-Interest

In this dialogue, Mark expresses his sympathy for an egoistic theory of human nature and an egoistic answer to the question concerning how we ought to live. He finds that the others have little sympathy for either psychological egoism or ethical egoism. At the end of the dialogue, a mysterious stranger, Donovan, appears.

MARK: Peter, Bob and I were chatting as we hiked today. You're having an effect on us. I don't know whether it's bad or good, but I'll say this, we've never talked about philosophy when we've played golf together.

BOB: Go on, Mark, tell him what we were talking about. I want to hear what the good professor has to say about it.

MARK: Oh, it's not that important.

BOB: Of course it is. We were talking about how we ought to live, what we should do with our lives. We were talking about America and the kind of people you find in the business world—at least some of them. And we were talking about a whole generation of people who have gone out into the world and seem to have this view that . . . no, you tell him.

PETER: Please go ahead, Mark. Does this have something to do with our previous conversations?

MARK: Probably. I was telling Bob today that I wish my best friend from the firm was here. He's very argumentative, very sharp. And very well-read. Opinionated. Has his own views of things. He says things that make a lot of sense to me.

BOB: Like?

MARK: Like what he says about selfishness and having to live your own life. He's a big fan of Ayn Rand.

SARAH: Who?

PETER: Ayn Rand, the writer. She came here from Russia after the revolution. Her most famous books were two large novels, *The Fountainhead* and *Atlas Shrugged*, although she has written many other books and essays espousing her philosophical views.

SARAH: She's a philosopher?

PETER: Of sorts. She had no academic credentials and she's never been taken too seriously by professional philosophers, but she does have a following, or at least at one time she did. My impression is that her influence has waned; now far fewer people read her books.

MARK: My friend Hunter does. He quotes her all the time.

RANSOM: What does she say?

MARK: Something like this: The problem we have in society is that people want you to be so concerned about others that you're supposed to be guilty when you act just for yourself. But what's really the most important thing in your life? Your own happiness. Does it really make any sense to sacrifice yourself for others? It's as if people look down on you if you're selfish. But why put others' happiness before your own? And isn't that what social morality asks you to do? Isn't that what we've been saying? What about personal morality? What about your own life? Just look at other people. Society wants you to work for others, and says you should feel guilty if you happen to have a good job, make a lot of money, and want the finer things in life for yourself. But everyone is trying to get all they can get out of life. Everyone is really out for themselves in the end. Even social workers and doctors and all the people who supposedly help others get satisfaction from what they do. They want pleasure and happiness for themselves. So what's wrong with it?

BOB: Are you sure that's Hunter's philosophy, or yours?

MARK: I said it makes a lot of sense to me.

SOPHIA: Sounds to me like the yuppie national anthem. Why not have it all? Now! Get it all while you can. Climb the corporate ladder, buy that BMW, the big house in the burbs, haute cuisine, ski trips to Aspen. Six figure income or bust! Who cares if a few people are hurt along the way? Only moral schmucks are still interested in poverty, hunger, and a more just society. Right?

ROSE: Calm down, Sophia.

SARAH: What kind of car do you have, Mark?

MARK: I happen to have a BMW. It's a fine car and I'm proud of it, not guilty about it.

SARAH: I'd be proud of it, too, if I could afford one. I don't see anything wrong with that.

SOPHIA: And don't forget, dress for success! We have to dress well to feel good about ourselves. Image is *so* important, isn't it?

BOB: Please, Sophia. We can discuss this seriously without the personal attacks.

SOPHIA: What exactly is it that I'm supposed to be serious about?

PETER: I don't think we can be so cavalier in our rejection of Mark's friend's point of view. There are serious and interesting issues involved in what he's said. They also relate to our previous discussions.

RANSOM: How's that?

PETER: Well, ethics involves a philosophical examination of human conduct. It investigates how we ought to act, what we ought to do. Mark, it seems to me, has expressed a full-blown ethical theory and perhaps even a view of human nature that is inconsistent with the great ethical theories of which I am aware—perhaps it's even incompatible with *any* ethical theory.

BOB: Tell us what you mean by "ethical theory"?

PETER: In my understanding, an ethical theory is an attempt somehow to systematize our moral beliefs. We carry around with us a ragged assortment of moral beliefs. We believe that certain types of action are morally right and others are morally wrong. We believe that certain traits of character are virtues. We believe that certain moral rules serve to guide our actions and help us decide what to do. Ethical theories attempt to provide some unity or coherence in our moral life, by asking the kinds of questions that will enable us to have a more general understanding of the particularities of moral life. For example, typically an ethical theory attempts to answer the question, what makes a right act right? What is the essence of rightness, so to speak? What is the basic principle which underlies all right action or correct moral rules? I believe Mark, or Mark's friend, has given an answer to these questions. He has given us a unifying vision of how we ought to go about living our life.

RANSOM: Which is?

PETER: Mark?

MARK: I suppose it's that people have a right to live their own lives and not feel guilty about it.

SARAH: That doesn't sound too controversial.

PETER: But why? Isn't there a deeper moral principle involved? Why do people have this right, and what is it, therefore, that they *ought* to do in life? What was the first idea you expressed? What, for you, is the greatest good in life?

MARK: My own happiness.

PETER: Then what ought you to do in life?

MARK: Pursue my own happiness.

PETER: And what ought I to do in life? Should I pursue *your* happiness?

MARK: No, not at all. That's not what I'm saying. I'm saying that you have every right to pursue your own happiness and I have every right to pursue mine.

PETER: So my good is most important for me, your good for you, and so forth. So there is a kind of impartiality in your view, in the sense that you're not saying that the whole world should act for you. Recall that we said that impartiality seems required when we reason ethically.

SOPHIA: But that's very strange. I thought impartiality meant something like seeing that others' interests are equal to my own, and that I must consider the interests of others when I act. Now this yuppie philosophy says I should only consider my own interests when I act. That seems contrary to what we've called the moral point of view.

PETER: I merely said that it was a *kind* of impartiality, so as to distinguish it from the absurd principle that everyone should act to promote *my* good, or *my* self-interest. That would be a quite silly ethical principle. Mark's principle is not that silly and it should be discussed seriously. What is his principle?

BOB: Everyone should act to promote his own good. That's your ethical principle, isn't it?

MARK: I suppose so.

PETER: It could be formulated in a variety of ways, but the main idea is this: Since each person's happiness is the highest good for him, every person ought to act to promote his own self-interest, or to maximize his own good. That view is typically called *ethical egoism*, to distinguish it from another kind of egoism that I also heard Mark espousing. Mark, didn't you say that everyone is basically selfish, that everyone seeks his own satisfaction or pleasure whenever he or she acts?

MARK: That's what Hunter believes and that's why he thinks there is so much hypocrisy in society. Why be guilty if everyone is basically selfish?

PETER: That view of human nature is usually called *psychological egoism*. It is also formulated in a variety of ways, as if each person always acts to maximize his own good, or that we all necessarily, always act from motivations of self-interest.

SARAH: Say that again. What's the difference between what you're calling psychological egoism and . . . what was it?

RANSOM: Ethical egoism.

PETER: That difference is this: One is a theory of human nature that attempts to *describe* how we do, in fact, act, that describes, supposedly, the central motivation underlying all of our action. The other is an ethical theory that *prescribes* how we ought to act, that is, that everyone *ought* to attempt to maximize his self-interest. The psychological thesis attempts to *explain* human action; the ethical theory, if successful, would *justify* self-interested action.

BOB: I thought we were talking about ethics, not psychology.

PETER: As a matter of fact, in my ethics class we do discuss psychological egoism, since it appears to be particularly relevant when thinking about the moral sphere of human existence. Do you see why?

BOB: I'm not sure.

PETER: Anyone? Ask yourself this question: What would be the consequences for morality if psychological egoism were true? Recall, morality attempts to say something about what we ought to do.

MARK: Well, if we can do nothing but what is in our self-interest, no one should be guilty for being selfish. You can't be guilty for what you can't help doing. It's just human nature.

SOPHIA: But if that is true, if we always just try to do what's best for ourselves, why do you also hold that everyone *ought* to act to maximize her own self-interest? If psychological egoism is true, we must all be doing exactly what we ought to do. That's a paradox.

MARK: But we could be mistaken about what's really in our interest. Even though we do have selfish motives, sometimes we're mistaken about what's best for us. If the psychological position is true, then what Peter calls "ethical egoism" can be the only acceptable ethical viewpoint.

BOB: No. I'd put it differently. I don't think it's a paradox; I think it's a contradiction. If we must *necessarily* pursue our self-interest, how could it make sense to say that we *ought* to pursue our self-interest? In fact, how could it make sense to say we *ought* to do anything? Psychological egoism is a form of determinism, isn't it Peter? And to say we ought to do a certain act must presuppose that we're free, that we have a choice between alternatives.

PETER: Quite so. As Kant held, "Ought implies can." To say we ought to do something is to imply that we *can* do it, that we're free to do it, as Bob said. It appears that the descriptive form of egoism says that as a matter of psychological necessity, we are only motivated to act from reasons of self-interest. So it is incompatible with the "ought" of morality. In particular, if moral motivation is essentially involved with acting on the basis of impartial reasons or principles, like the Golden Rule, for example, then if psychological egoism is true it would appear that we could never be motivated to act morally, that is, impartially. So it's very important for ethical reflection to consider whether moral motivation is even possible.

ANTHONY: This is very interesting. Don't get me wrong, I'm not an egoist. But it occurs to me that the egoist could hold his doctrine and if he could show that acting morally or acting for others *is* in a person's self-interest then the "ought" would make sense. In that case, he could say we ought to be moral because it's best for us, and he could hold that position consistently even if his psychological determinism were true.

PETER: Very interesting. Somewhat like Mark's earlier point that there might be a difference between what a person *is* doing and what he *ought* to do because he is confused about his self-interest.

ANTHONY: That does happen often, doesn't it? Sometimes people are impulsive; they act on instinct instead of what's best for them in the long run.

BOB: That's a cagey move, but it works only if you could convince a person that it's always in his interest to do the morally right thing.

PETER: Example?

SOPHIA: Sometimes people make great sacrifices for others; they even lose their lives because they want to do the right thing. A soldier drops on a grenade to save others, or parents make sacrifices for their children. Remember the stories about the prison camps in World War II. People would refuse to help the Nazis gas others, even if that help would have been necessary to save themselves.

SARAH: But now we're back to the original question, because Mark says we're always selfish. Even those people are acting for themselves. Maybe that's right.

PETER: If we decide that such actions don't really serve the long-term interests of individuals, yet they are laudable from the moral point of view and they do occur, I think we'll see that psychological egoism would be a damaging doctrine if it were true, but it happens not to be, in my judgment.

SOPHIA: So it still turns on the issue of whether we are always self-interested or selfish.

PETER: Yes. Let's look at the evidence and consider some examples. Why does it appear plausible, at least to some?

ALICE: That's the easiest question you've asked since we started these philosophical conversations. Just look at people. They're out for themselves. That's what our economic system is all about, isn't it?

SARAH: Look at people who say they're trying to help others. Politicians do things, but they want to get reelected. They love power and fame. You should see the premed students at school. They say they want to help people, but then they do everything they can to make lots of money. Ransom here doesn't want to go to hell. That's self-interest.

ROSE: I want to say something now. I know there are people who are just interested in themselves, but I don't believe that's true for everyone. Some people are kind and loving and helpful. They give no thought to themselves and devote long hours and large parts of their lives to helping others.

SOPHIA: I agree. I think it's cynical and uncaring to think that everyone is really selfish. It sounds to me more like someone trying to rationalize his own selfish behavior by saying that everyone else does the same thing. So why be guilty? Look at people like Albert Schweitzer and Mother Teresa. Do you or your friend really believe that Mother Teresa is just acting for her own pleasure?

MARK: She's doing what she wants to do, or else she wouldn't be doing it at all. And it must make her happy, or she wouldn't do it. She's doing what she wants to do, just like all of us.

ROSE: But Mark, we don't always do what we want to do, do we? Last week I had to go to the hospital and visit a good friend of mine who is dying. I didn't want to do it. I made every excuse to myself to avoid doing it. But I went. I had to.

MARK: But why?

ROSE: Because she's my friend. I thought I owed her some of my time. I thought maybe I could do just a little something for her; she's done so much for me.

MARK: Didn't it make you feel good?

ROSE: No, not at all. In fact, I would say that I was depressed after I saw her. She has declined so rapidly. It was so sad.

MARK: But you wanted to do it.

ROSE: No, I didn't. I really didn't.

MARK: You did it, though.

PETER: May I interrupt here? It seems to me that egoist arguments typically confuse some issues. I'm not sure this will convince you, Mark, or your friend, but allow me to indicate the sorts of responses philosophers have made to these arguments.

MARK: Please do.

PETER: First, you say that Rose must have wanted to visit her friend, or else she wouldn't have gone. You seem to think that since action is motivated by personal desires, all desires must be self-directed, so to speak. But just because an action is self-motivated, it doesn't seem to follow that it is selfish. It's the intention, the purpose, of the act that makes it selfish or not, not the mere fact that the act is self-motivated. Self-motivation does not necessarily equal selfish motivation.

BOB: Give us an example.

PETER: There are really two questions here. If I decide to go to a restaurant to eat, that action is probably motivated by self-interest, but it's not *selfish* unless I act for myself and exclude considering others when I ought to. I might clip my toenails because they've grown too long and make my feet uncomfortable. That's not "selfish" behavior, is it? It is, in a broad sense, self-interested. So the first point to be made is that the egoist, in holding that all behavior is selfish, simply confuses self-interest and selfishness. They're not the same.

MARK: All right, I see that.

PETER: Furthermore, if the object or intent of the desire makes it selfish, or self-directed, not the mere presence of a desire, then there's no reason to think that all desires *are* self-interested. Rose had a desire *to help her friend*. She wanted to do an act that comforted her friend and helped her in the dying process. That appears to be a self-motivated act that is neither selfish nor self-interested. That's a clear counterexample to psychological egoism.

MARK: But it gave Rose some pleasure or happiness to help her friend. It made her feel good.

ROSE: I already said it didn't.

PETER: Again, there are two points. Suppose someone asks me for directions and I give them. You say, ah, it made you feel good. But I insist that nothing of that kind happened. Someone asked for directions, and I gave them. I didn't feel anything at all. Why do you insist you know how I *really* feel? It seems to me that the egoist is in the odd position of claiming to know my mental state, or Rose's mental state, better than I do or Rose does. Moreover, suppose unselfish or other-directed behavior *does* make someone feel satisfied. Suppose Mother Teresa *does* derive satisfaction from helping others. Does that mean that she was really motivated by seeking her own pleasure? Not at all. The satisfaction she derives is the surest sign of unselfishness, since it arises when her other-directed desires are satisfied. Pleasure or satisfaction isn't the *object* of the desire; it is the *consequence* of its satisfaction. If a person gains satisfaction from doing something, it doesn't follow that it is done simply for the sake of satisfaction. For example, I have derived a great deal of satisfaction from studying philosophy, but that's not why I began or continue to study philosophy. I wanted to learn, I wanted to think about the great philosophical issues confronting us.

SARAH: Professor, I love it when you get cranked up.

PETER: I'm sorry. I shouldn't dominate the conversation.

ANTHONY: Not at all. So what's the bottom line?

PETER: Most philosophers have felt that psychological egoism is the result of a nest of confusions. We appear to have all kinds of motivations in life. We do things in order to learn, to create, to question, to enjoy, to change things, to escape boredom, to share. . . . One could go on and on. And sometimes, often, it appears that we act to try to do the morally right thing, sometimes to help others, sometimes to do our duty or to fulfill our obligations. It would be quite startling, wouldn't it, if we could reduce all human motivation to just one category? I suspect that our experience is much more complex than that.

BOB: We still have the ethical position to consider, don't we? What about *ethical* egoism? It sounds to me like an immoral doctrine.

SOPHIA: Sounds to me like yuppiedom in a microcosm.

SARAH: Say again what ethical egoism is.

PETER: It is the view that everyone ought to act to maximize her self-interest. It holds that what makes an act right for an agent is whether the act produces the best long-term consequences for her.

SARAH: It doesn't sound that radical. I can see why you think it makes a lot of sense, Mark.

PETER: Why do you think it makes sense, Sarah?

SARAH: Sometimes I think we'd all be better off if we simply minded our own business and didn't stick our noses into other people's lives.

SOPHIA: If what you're saying is that the world would be better off if we were all egoists, I just don't believe that. It seems to me that the opposite is probably nearer the truth. You've heard about a "kinder and gentler America"? You don't need to sell egoism to the Ku Klux Klan, skinheads, yuppie narcissists, inside traders, and cocaine dealers. They're already trying to maximize their self-interest, and I don't think we're all better off for it.

MARK: It's not that easy. If we want to do what's best for our long-run interests, we don't break the law and cause social disruption.

BOB: I still don't see what the major argument is for ethical egoism.

MARK: It's very simple. Our own happiness is most important for each one of us. Why should we sacrifice that for others? Does that really make sense? Do we really appreciate the value and the integrity of the *individual* if we sacrifice ourselves for others?

PETER: That does sound like Ayn Rand's position, as if acting to maximize one's self-interest is clearly the most *rational* guide in life, in some sense of "rational."

BOB: What sense of "rational"?

PETER: Mark?

MARK: Better help me on that one.

PETER: It's a kind of instrumental rationality. We all have goals or purposes when we act. Rationality, for some, is finding the best way to achieve our goals. In that sense, it would be quite literally "irrational" if we acted in such a way as to thwart our goals or purposes or we acted stupidly in trying to achieve our purposes.

SOPHIA: But what about the question of the rationality of the goals themselves? That's not the same question, and that must be a different sense of "rationality."

PETER: Very good point. We still wonder how to choose our values, not simply what is the best way to achieve our goals, once we have decided what to pursue. However, Mark insists that it's only ethical egoism that preserves the value or dignity of the individual. Is that right?

MARK: That's what Hunter says. Altruism says that you have to sacrifice yourself for others in life. Egoism says it's rational to pursue your own happiness.

PETER: I must say that it is precisely at this point that most philosophers have found Ayn Rand's doctrine either simplistic or even confused.

BOB: Why?

PETER: Because of the way she casts the alternatives. She seems to think there are only two fundamental alternatives in life: either pursue your own interests exclusively or sacrifice your interests to the interests of others. She appears to think that altruism is what we've called the moral point of view, as if you're either a rugged individualist ruthlessly pursuing your own happiness or you're a kind of moral doormat, devoting your life exclusively to others. But it seems to me that those are *not* the only two alternatives. Surely your own life is important morally; it's just that it counts for no more than another person's. You have every right, in fact you're required, morally, to respect yourself, not to allow yourself to be used or exploited for the happiness of others, to count your own interests as important as others'. Morality doesn't require you to sacrifice yourself for others. It demands only a certain equality, that you *do* consider others' interests when you act, and you not harm others just to achieve your own goals.

MARK: But that is still the problem. If I accept equality, it means that I believe your happiness is as important as mine, for me. Can we really accept that?

PETER: Let's do this. Let's suppose we accept your fundamental ethical principle. Let's suppose it is the basic guide to our actions in life. One of the ways to understand and even to test a theory is to see whether it is consistent and to see what the consequences of accepting the theory would be. Let's see what it implies and attempt to judge whether we would be prepared to accept such consequences.

MARK: All right. I assume you have something in mind.

PETER: Let's suppose we are acquaintances, or even friends, and we find ourselves competing for the same job. Suppose we both have a family, we've been laid off for some time, the bills are mounting, our marriages are becoming shaky, and the job is one we would highly enjoy. Now suppose that we each have a chance to spread an ugly false rumor about the other, and we each have a chance to falsify our credentials to enhance our chances of getting the job.

MARK: Okay.

PETER: Now suppose you're an ethical egoist. You hold that everyone should act to maximize his self-interest. What ought you to do?

BOB: It's clear that the ethical egoist should cheat and lie about his friend.

PETER: What should his friend do, or rather, what should the egoist *want* his friend to do?

SARAH: If he wants the job, he should want his friend to be a good guy and not lie about him.

PETER: But remember, his doctrine says that *everyone* should attempt to maximize his own good.

SOPHIA: I see what you're getting at. Can he really have it both ways? The egoist wants the job, so he must be willing to lie and cheat. But he also holds that his friend ought to pursue his own good, so he must want his friend to lie and cheat to get the job. How can he want both things?

PETER: Quite right. How can he? Philosophers have wondered whether the doctrine is coherent. Or, to put it somewhat differently, let's suppose the egoist knows about the competitive situation, his friend does not, and his friend comes to the egoist for advice about whether to compete for the job the egoist wants. Let's suppose that if the friend does attempt to get the job he will probably be successful (perhaps the egoist has inside information) and it will be important for his happiness. What ought the egoist to tell his friend?

SOPHIA: Well, if the egoist wants to maximize his own good, he ought to tell his friend *not* to try to get the job.

PETER: But his doctrine is that everyone ought to pursue his own good. To be consistent, it seems that he must tell his friend to compete for the job. But that's not in the egoist's interest. How can he be consistent here? In fact, if he does want his friend to avoid applying for the job, it appears that he is really holding that his friend ought to act to maximize the *egoist's* good. Now he seems to have reduced himself to the absurd doctrine that people ought to act to achieve the egoist's good, and that doesn't seem at all fair. He's arbitrarily placing his own good above the good of others.

BOB: So the problems arise when there are conflicting interests. How are these conflicting interests to be resolved, from the egoistic point of view?

PETER: That's a very difficult quesiton, isn't it Mark?

MARK: Why do you think they have to be resolved?

PETER: That's at least one thing that philosophers have often held to be essential to morality, that it is a perspective that attempts to resolve conflicts.

SOPHIA: I believe that I see another curiosity here. Mark, why would you want to convince us of the truth of your ethical doctrine if you're an egoist?

MARK: What do you mean?

SOPHIA: If our interests *do* conflict, as they inevitably must if we live in a society with limited goods, then it isn't in your self-interest to convince us to pursue our self-interest and neglect yours. You shouldn't be advocating your doctrine publicly.

SARAH: That's weird.

PETER: No, it's simply another uncomfortable result of ethical egoism. It doesn't seem that it can be consistently publicly advocated. To maximize his own interests, the egoist should probably advocate that people should be as caring and helpful and trustworthy as possible, because that will help the egoist in the long run. But the egoist should secretly pursue his own good, exclusively. It's dishonest. Again, it's not clear that he can consistently hold that *everyone* should do what he does, and that was supposedly one of the sources of the viewpoint's plausibility.

BOB: If that's the case, then why not just say, flat-out, that it's an immoral doctrine? Take your example again, Peter. If ethical egoism says it's permissible to lie and cheat to get the job, then it's an immoral doctrine. If you want to kill your elderly relative to gain an inheritance and you can get away with it, egoism says "go ahead." If you can embezzle money and escape to the Riviera for the rest of your life, then that's all right, according to the egoist.

PETER: Those are precisely the kinds of counterexamples that philosophers have used to refute ethical egoism. Apart from the problems of consistency, or giving moral advice, or publicly advocating the doctrine, many have said that it is simply morally vicious if it would allow you to do these things in the pursuit of your own interests.

MARK: But would it? A person might get caught. There's always that chance. And a person would feel guilty if he did these things. Those things might not be in the long-term interests of the egoist.

SOPHIA: Why feel guilty? If you were a consistent egoist, you wouldn't have any basis for guilt since you would think you're doing the right thing.

BOB: But not the *morally* right thing. And some people might not get caught.

PETER: At the very least, ethical egoism would seem to condone all kinds of immoral acts *if* they are done secretly, *if* they cause no negative psychological consequences, and *if* they enhance the life of the agent. It is rather more complicated, however. I can imagine that the egoist might still have a comeback.

SARAH: You have the stage, Professor.

PETER: This is the point that has sometimes bothered me. I think it is at least somewhat plausible that it is in our long-term interest to live a moral life. If we try to be good people, if we teach our children to be good, if we reinforce the goodness of others, our own life may be less difficult and more satisfying. So perhaps ethical egoism can be seen, not as an evil ethical doctrine, but as the ultimate answer to the question "Why be moral?" Because it is in our long-term interest.

SOPHIA: Another paradox, Professor?

PETER: I'm not sure I'd call it a paradox. Perhaps we could say that we've reached an interesting sort of dilemma. Either ethical egoism is obviously false as a moral doctrine, because it advocates that we can perform immoral acts in the pursuit of our own good, or it is not a moral doctrine at all. Perhaps it's the standpoint *outside* of morality that challenges us to ask the question "Why be moral at all?" Why should we live a *moral* life, that is, a life in which we always consider the effects of our actions on the lives of others, and in which we consider moral reasons as crucial for deciding how we ought to act? Perhaps, as some have held, the ultimate rationale for morality concerns an appeal to the flourishing of each individual.

DONOVAN: Too easy, Professor.

At this point the group is startled by a voice from the darkness beyond the camp fire. A large rugged-looking man appears, with a full beard, dressed in warm clothes and mountain boots. He walks over to Peter and stares at him, silent for a moment.

DONOVAN: And life is never as simple as you academic *philosophers* make it. You sift it through your analytical brains, you run it through your arguments, your rational justifications, your precise distinctions, and it comes out without any edges. It comes out nice and neat, with all the "false" doctrines perfectly refuted, and the peacefulness of ordinary life restored for the herd. Isn't that right, Peter? Isn't that what we learned in graduate school?

PETER: Not exactly, Donovan. That's not how I would put it.

DONOVAN: Still doing ethics, my friend? Still putting "theories" to the test? I've been listening. You have some fine pupils here. They catch on very quickly. And you've led them to the "proper" conclusions, no doubt.

PETER: You, Donovan? What are you doing these days? Where's your home?

DONOVAN: This is my home. These mountains are my home. You're trespassing.

PETER: No more philosophy?

DONOVAN: No more philosophy, but much more thinking than when I lived down there. So you've done away with the problem of egoism for these people. Perhaps another theory tomorrow? Maybe utilitarianism, eh? Have we resolved these knotty issues? Morality is overriding, authoritative, demanding—equality, universalizability, weighing the interests of others, avoiding arbitrariness. Preserve the "common" judgment that saints like Schweitzer and Mother Teresa are our ideals. They're so *perfectly* good. How boring! How perfectly boring! Have you told them about other personal ideals? Have you mentioned the primacy of individual perfection? Have you talked about Gauguin as well as Mother Teresa?

PETER: Or Nietzsche?

DONOVAN: Yes, Nietzsche, of course.

PETER: And power? The weakness of Christian, slave morality? The silliness of helping others, turning the other cheek, sympathy, pity, and *ressentiment?*

DONOVAN: Still not so easy, Peter. Don't slot me into the simple Nietzschean category. I learned a great deal from Nietzsche, but I've learned a great deal from others. [He turns to the group and smiles.] Actually, I'm thrilled to see my old friend. . . . But I'm being impolite. A vice, Peter? I've lost all sense of civility up here in the mountains. Forgive me. [He begins to walk away.]

PETER: Donovan! You're not going so soon.

DONOVAN: I'm sure I'll be back. Especially if I hear the *chatter* of philosophy. It's irresistible. [He walks into the darkness.]

SOPHIA: Very strange. Will you tell us about your friend, Peter?

PETER: One of the brightest, most interesting people I met in graduate school. He stayed for three years and left. Traveled. I lost track of him. I hope he'll visit us again. You would enjoy talking to him.

SOPHIA: Yes, I think I would.

What Thinkers Have Said

Now whatsoever seems good, is pleasant, and relates either to the senses, or the mind. But all the mind's pleasure is either glory, (or to have a good opinion of one's self), or refers to glory in the end; the rest are sensual, or conducing to sensuality, which may be all comprehended under the word conveniences. All society therefore is either for gain, or for glory; that is, not so much for love of our fellows, as for the love of ourselves.

Thomas Hobbes, *Philosophical Rudiments Concerning Government and Society*

Whosoever therefore holds, that it had been best to have continued in that state in which all things were lawful for all men, he contradicts himself. For every man by natural necessity desires that which is good for him: nor is there any that esteems a war of all against all, which necessarily adheres to such a state, to be good for him. And so it happens, that through fear of each other we think it fit to rid ourselves of this condition, and to get some fellows; that if there needs must be war, it may not yet be against all men, nor without some helps.

Thomas Hobbes, *Philosophical Rudiments Concerning Government and Society*

If it is true that what I mean by "selfishness" is not what is meant conventionally, then this is one of the worst indictments of altruism: it means that altruism permits no concept of a self-respecting, self-supporting man—a man who supports his life by his own effort and neither sacrifices himself nor others. It means that altruism permits no view of men except as sacrificial animals and profiteers-on-sacrifice, as victims and parasites—that it permits no concept of a benevolent co-existence among men—that it permits no concept of justice. . . .

To rebel against so devastating an evil, one has to rebel against its basic premise. To redeem both man and morality, it is the concept of "selfishness" that one has to redeem.

Ayn Rand, *The Virtue of Selfishness*

The Objectivist ethics holds that the actor must always be the beneficiary of his action and that man must act for his own rational self-interest. But his right to do so is derived from his nature as man and from the function of moral values in human life—and, therefore, is applicable only in the context of a rational, objectively demonstrated and validated code of moral principles which define and determine his actual self-interest. It is not a license "to do as he pleases" and it is not applicable to the altruists' image of a "selfish" brute nor to any man motivated by irrational emotions, feelings, urges, wishes or whims.

Ayn Rand, *The Virtue of Selfishness*

Everyone is selfish; everyone is doing what he believes will make himself happier. The recognition of that can take most of the sting out of accusations that you're being "selfish." Why should you feel guilty for seeking your own happiness when that's what everyone else is doing, too?

The demand that you be unselfish can be motivated by any number of reasons: that you'd help create a better world, that you have a moral obligation to be unselfish, that you give up your happiness to the selfishness of someone else, or that the person demanding it has just never thought it out.

Whatever the reason, you're not likely to convince such a person to stop his demands. But it will create much less pressure on you if you realize that it's his selfish reason. And you can eliminate the problem entirely by looking for more compatible companions.

Harry Browne, "The Morality Trap"

Key Terms and Concepts

ethical theory

altruism

ethical egoism

conflicting interests

psychological egoism

moral advice

self-interest vs. selfishness

immoral doctrine

self-directed vs. other-directed

why be moral?

Questions

1. Explain the difference between psychological egoism and ethical egoism.

2. How does the psychological egoist respond to the obvious counterexamples to his position? Do you find his response convincing? If he accepts no possible counterexample, if his theory cannot in principle be falsified, what kind of theory does he really hold?

3. Explain the distinction between self-motivation and selfish motivation. Why is this distinction important in critically evaluating psychological egoism?

4. When a person acts on the basis of self-destructive compulsion, is it correct to say that the person is motivated by self-interest? What if the person knows that his compulsion is self-destructive but cannot change his behavior?

5. What are the consequences for moral education, if ethical egoism is accepted? Do you find such consequences acceptable?

6. Do you think ethical egoism is an immoral doctrine? Why or why not?

7. Do you believe that an acceptable ethical theory must be able to be espoused publicly? If I were an ethical egoist, should I publicly espouse Ayn Rand's doctrine or ethical altruism?

Suggested Readings

Browne, Harry, *How I Found Freedom in an Unfree World*, Macmillan, 1937. The source of the quotation above.

Butler, Joseph, *Fifteen Sermons Preached at Rolls Chapel*, Oxford, 1726. Classic criticism of psychological egoism.

Feinberg, Joel, "Psychological Egoism," *Reason and Responsibility*, Wadsworth, 1985. Superb discussion of central arguments against psychological egoism.

Hobbes, Thomas, *Leviathan*, Michael Oakeshott, ed., Oxford, 1947. The famous philosopher most commonly associated with egoism.

Hobbes, Thomas, *Philosophical Rudiments Concerning Government and Society*, in *An Introduction to Ethics*, ed. by Dewey and Hurlbutt, Macmillan, 1977.

MacIntyre, Alasdair, "Egoism and Altruism," in *The Encyclopedia of Philosophy*, ed. Paul Edwards, Macmillan, 1967. Informative historical treatment.

Rachels, James, *The Elements of Moral Philosophy*, chs. 5 and 6, Random House, 1986. Entertaining summary of psychological egoism; excellent critical response to Ayn Rand's defense of ethical egoism.

Rand, Ayn, *The Virtue of Selfishness*, New America Library, 1964. An enthusiastic defense of ethical egoism.

Dialogue Five:
Ethics and Consequences

In this dialogue, the backpackers discuss utilitarianism. After initially favorable comments, numerous objections are raised, including the problem of justice. Donovan once again appears and aggressively criticizes utilitarianism as an extraordinarily demanding ethical doctrine.

SOPHIA: A very strange end to our conversation last night. I couldn't quite tell what your old friend was getting at. What's his name?

PETER: Donovan.

SOPHIA: Yes, Donovan. Interesting. Obviously, he's studied some philosophy. I couldn't tell whether he was bitter, angry, alienated, ironic . . . Do you think he'll be back?

PETER: Very difficult to say.

BOB: He did say that if we talked about philosophy he might pop in. I don't think we should disappoint him.

SARAH: Can't get enough, can you, Bob?

BOB: I told you about my two most recently acquired loves: philosophy and the mountains. I do have a question, Peter. You haven't grown tired of us, have you?

PETER: Not at all.

BOB: Well, I see a kind of logical progression in our conversations about ethics. I was talking to Mark about this today. After we talked the first night about what ethics is, we considered some fairly common ways to get at ethical questions. We tried to define ethics in terms of religion, then in terms of society. Both tried to appeal to some kind of authority, one religious and one social. The problem was pretty clear: Just because God or society says something is right doesn't make it so. We have to judge that our God's commands and our society's moral rules are ethically acceptable, and for that we need to use our judgment, our own powers of reasoning. That's what you argued, at least.

PETER: All right.

BOB: Then we talked about Mark's egoist friend and we decided, I think, that ethics doesn't involve just trying to get your own good. It must also consider others' good. But you can also take yourself into account. You need not act solely for others and ignore yourself.

PETER: Quite good. The ethical egoist says everyone should attempt to maximize his own good, but this can lead to morally unacceptable acts. The ethical altruist supposedly says act *only* to promote the interests of others. That's the person I called a "moral doormat."

BOB: The alternative to these two is clear, isn't it?

SARAH: Is it?

BOB: Yes, but I have bad associations with it, for some reason. The logical alternative is utilitarianism, isn't it, Peter? We spent some sessions talking about it at the institute, and what I remember best is a long discussion about "cost-benefit analyses" and "do the ends justify the means?"

SOPHIA: Slow down, Mortimer. Donovan mentioned utilitarianism, didn't he? With *not* a nice tone in his voice, either.

ANTHONY: If what you're talking about involves cost-benefit analyses, I can tell you some things about some government studies I've been involved with.

SARAH: What's that got to do with morality?

BOB: Quite a bit, I think. As I recall, utilitarianism says that we should promote the greatest happiness of the greatest number of people.

SARAH: That's what utilitarianism says? I've heard of that, but I thought utilitarianism is just being practical or pragmatic.

PETER: Bob is right. Utilitarianism has a specific meaning in philosophy. It's a moral theory that was developed in the eighteenth century by the British philosopher Jeremy Bentham and was given its most famous expression and defense by John Stuart Mill in the nineteenth century. It continues to be talked about and defended in contemporary thought as one of the most powerful general accounts of what morality is about and what morality requires from us. I think you can see why many find it so plausible, especially if you compare it to ethical egoism and ethical altruism, as Bob has. Egoists consider only their own interests; altruists, at least theoretically, consider only others' interests. Utilitarians want us to consider *everyone's* interests when we act, including our own.

SOPHIA: I can certainly see one strength right away. If morality requires us to be impartial, then utilitarianism sounds like it fits the bill.

PETER: Yes. If we simply extend to others what the egoist wants for himself, we easily arrive at the utilitarian viewpoint. Utilitarianism says that, from the moral point of view, my interests count no more than anyone else's. There's the equality. It insists that moral judgments are impersonal, in this sense. What we ought to do when we act is to produce the best results for everyone involved.

SARAH: That still sounds pragmatic.

PETER: But the utilitarian has a quite specific understanding of what would constitute the best results. The best results consist in maximizing overall good or happiness for all those affected by the act. Utilitarianism says, quite simply, that we should try to maximize good and minimize evil when we act. Morally, we ought to make the world better by attempting to bring about the best state of affairs we can.

SARAH: Sounds good to me.

PETER: Ransom, you'll be pleased to hear that Mill claimed that Jesus' teachings about "doing unto others" and "love your neighbor as yourself" were the perfect embodiment of utilitarian morality.

BOB: If I understand this right, utilitarianism says that it's just the consequences that are important. Right? Always produce the best consequences.

PETER: Yes. It is sometimes called *consequentialism*, since the evaluation of moral action rests solely on judging the consequences of the act.

SARAH: So it does say the ends justify the means.

PETER: We need to be very careful here. Obviously, consequentialism says that the ends or the consequences of action are the basis for moral evaluation, but the means by which we attempt to bring about consequences will themselves have consequences, perhaps even bad ones. So it's simplistic to think that a utilitarian would sanction any kind of act so long as the results are good.

ROSE: I can see why philosophers like this theory. It says be considerate of others when you act and try to help people be as happy as possible. I can agree with that. That's what many people think anyway, don't they?

PETER: People do use utilitarian moral reasoning, if that's what you're suggesting. It's a very common way in which people go about making their moral decisions. It also seems to be particularly useful in public policy decisions. We need to know the consequences of certain social policies we're considering.

SARAH: Then what's the big deal? What's to criticize? What's the controversy?

PETER: There are a number of interesting practical and philosophical questions that arise when we think hard about utilitarianism. For example, many people who are otherwise sympathetic to it wonder whether it offers us a *complete* account of our obligations. Perhaps trying to produce as much good as possible is only part of the moral life.

ALICE: I can see one question right away.

PETER: Yes?

ALICE: How can we really know what the consequences of our actions are? Can we really determine the effects of our actions? Sometimes we think we're doing the right thing, and the results turn out terribly. I can see what utilitarianism is getting at. For example, in the public schools we often have problem children who disrupt classrooms and cause a lot of problems. We have to try to do the best thing for everyone concerned, but it's so difficult to know whether you've done the right thing. We have to consider the child's family, his future life, his capabilities, as well as all the children in the normal classroom who are affected by the behavior.

PETER: Perhaps you've answered your own question. Can we accurately predict consequences? Do we reason this way? Are you ever satisfied that you've done the right thing?

ALICE: As I've said, it's difficult to make these predictions, but sometimes, . . . no, often, I think we're able to get the best results. We base our judgment on psychological tests, we talk to many people, and we make judgments based on past experience.

PETER: I'm not sure we can do better than that. Most consequentialists would admit that there are uncertainties and ambiguities involved when we attempt to evaluate the consequences of actions. We shouldn't overestimate the precision or the accuracy of our judgments. But very often in life, it seems to me, we *are* well prepared to make sound judgments about the results of our action. If Rose goes to see her friend in the hospital, she assumes that her friend will be comforted. If we punish our children, we think it will have a positive effect on their future behavior. If we give to United Way, we believe that our charitable contributions will help others.

ANTHONY: There's no doubt that governments have to try to predict consequences when they consider various social programs. For example, I think affirmative action programs have gotten many more people involved in worthwhile jobs and professions. I know they're controversial, but I believe the results have been positive.

MARK: But have they been fair? Hasn't there been reverse discrimination when some lesser-qualified minorities have gotten jobs because of quota systems?

RANSOM: The same thing has happened in universities. White males have been denied admission to medical schools, although blacks with lower test scores and grades have been admitted.

ANTHONY: Blacks have historically been the object of racism in this society. This infects all aspects of their lives, including their education, their family life, and even the standardized tests they have to take to "succeed" in white-dominated higher education. I see affirmative action as an equalizing tool, to allow minorities to compete more equally and produce a more just society where *all* people get a piece of the pie.

PETER: We may not agree on the arguments concerning preferential treatment programs, but that's a good example of utilitarian arguments being used and criticized. Is overall good maximized by preferential treatment programs? Are rights unfairly denied in the process? You see, Sarah, producing as much good as possible may not be the entire moral picture.

BOB: I see a number of problems, or at least questions. We talked about some of these at the institute.

PETER: Yes?

BOB: If utilitarianism says that we should try to produce the greatest happiness of the greatest number of people, there's a problem. It's ambiguous. Are we supposed to produce the greatest *happiness,* or the greatest happiness *of the greatest number?* Do you see the problem?

SARAH: I don't get it.

BOB: Okay. Suppose I have five thousand dollars to contribute to a local high school for college scholarships. Suppose I can choose to split up the money however I want to, but I want to do as much good as I can. Do I give one five thousand dollar scholarship to a very bright and needy student? Do I give ten five hundred dollar scholarships? Do I give five one thousand dollar scholarships? Or, to put it differently: Do I do much good for a smaller number of people or do I try to affect more people, even though I can't do as much for each or overall?

SOPHIA: Excellent question, Bob.

ALICE: It's also back to the issue of how would I know what produced the best consequences.

PETER: These are difficult issues for the consequentialist, but the answer he usually gives attempts to resolve the ambiguity in question. He wants to produce the greatest total good, as a whole, as an *aggregate*, as the utilitarian says. If, in his judgment, more good would be produced by doing much for a smaller number of people, or, in Bob's example, giving only one major scholarship, that's what he must do.

SARAH: Is that fair to the nine people who might not get any scholarship?

PETER: This is precisely where the utilitarian's calculations become more complicated. Bob would have to weigh the positive effects of giving one scholarship and the negative effects on the lives of those who might not receive a five hundred dollar grant.

BOB: So the doctrine isn't "greatest happiness of the greatest number of people." We're supposed to produce the greatest happiness, period.

PETER: Yes. The greatest total good, or the most utility, as philosophers might say, where utility is the total positive value of the consequences minus whatever negative effects, or disvalue, might occur as the result of the act.

BOB: I have another problem. Suppose I'm a utilitarian and I still have my five thousand dollars to contribute to high school seniors. Suppose ten students want to go to Europe for a year, just to hike around and have a good time. It would make them happy. How do I balance the pleasure they would get if I bought their airfare and the happiness of students who might use the money for a college education?

SOPHIA: Or what if a student needed a large chunk of money to start a drug business? Suppose his family is very poor, the father and mother are unemployed, and he could support the family by selling cocaine. Would I produce the greatest happiness by giving him money rather than the kids who want to go to Europe or the kids who want to continue their education?

PETER: This is an old problem for the utilitarian, but one he can probably handle if you are once again prepared to accept the inevitable ambiguities of moral decision making. In fact, Mill tried to respond to a similar objection in his book *Utilitarianism*. He held that we ought to attempt to promote the greatest happiness, and he held that happiness is equivalent to pleasure. Some thought that this was, as Mill expressed it, a "doctrine worthy of swine," as if we are no better than pigs if our goal in life is to produce as much pleasure as possible for ourselves and others. But his response is quite famous. I think the way he defended it was fraught with logical errors, but the basic insight appears to be sound. He said that it is better to be "Socrates dissatisfied than a pig satisfied." That is, he thought that some kinds of satisfactions or pleasures are "higher" than others. Some pleasures are qualitatively better than others.

SOPHIA: Like the satisfaction associated with going to college, learning new things, seeking knowledge, rather than taking a vacation or making money by dealing drugs.

PETER: Precisely. The European vacation might have some educational benefit, but on the face of it, if there are no other variables involved, the long-term good effects of a college education are greater than the European vacation. It's at least a reasonable assumption that greater happiness will result by aiding the pursuit of higher education. The potential drug dealer is handled in the same manner. First, there are numerous potential destructive consequences of the act. The dealer might be arrested and put in jail for years, he might be killed by competing drug dealers, the effects on those to whom he sells the cocaine are potentially destructive, and so forth.

BOB: But this whole business of producing the greatest happiness is so complex. How can we really define happiness? Peter, do you think it's just pleasure, as Mill said?

PETER: Mill got himself involved in all kinds of problems with his doctrine that the highest good is pleasure and that there are "higher" and "lower" pleasures. First, I totally agree with him that some satisfactions in life are "better" than others, in *some* sense. But one of his big problems is that he wanted to assert both that pleasure is the sole value in life—that doctrine is called hedonism—and that some pleasures are *better* than others. The puzzle is clear. If some pleasures are better than others, what would be the basis for saying that, if you also hold that pleasure is the sole value in life? He wanted to defend his doctrine by insisting that pleasures differ in *quality* as well as quantity, but what would be that standard by which to make such a claim?

BOB: You're saying that he must hold that something besides pleasure makes one better than another, but then pleasure isn't the sole value in life.

PETER: Or, and at least this is the consistent answer, he could hold that the differences aren't really qualitative at all. The reason that education is so important concerns the long-term benefits. The *quantity* of satisfaction throughout life that is produced by education. It broadens our interests, it makes us more sensitive, it provides escape from the narrowness and even boredom of a life whose concerns are quite limited.

ANTHONY: To beer, baseball, and fishing.

PETER: Yes. There is a much deeper problem, however. Is pleasure the sole value in life? Is pleasure what makes everything else in life valuable? That is, ought we to accept hedonism as the theory of value that consequentialism is based on? I don't think so, and an ingenious thought experiment shows this.

SOPHIA: A thought experiment?

PETER: Sometimes philosophers have created imaginative situations that we believe aren't actually true, but could be. These situations sometimes show us interesting perspectives on certain philosophical issues. Do you remember Descartes's famous thought experiment?

BOB: The evil genius?

PETER: Yes. What if a God existed, just as powerful as the one many people believe in, but one bent on deceiving me about everything I see and think about? What could I really *know* if that were true? And if "knowing" means being certain there is no evil genius, then can we really claim to *know* anything at all? His thought experiment captured in an ingenious way the absolute character of claiming to know, that is, being certain about our beliefs. If we can't prove there is no evil genius deceiving us, or perhaps some race of powerful alien beings experimenting on us, perhaps we can't claim to *know* anything at all.

SARAH: I remember that in the early morning fog of my philosophy class. Bizarre!

BOB: What about hedonism?

PETER: This thought experiment has been put in a couple of different ways. Suppose we have available to us a "pleasure machine" or an "experience machine." Suppose we can hook ourselves up to this machine indefinitely and we can experience the very pleasures associated with all the things in life that do bring satisfaction to us. Suppose the experience machine requires that you float in a large tank of water with electrodes attached to your brain, and you can have all the experiences or pleasures associated with sex, food, drink, friendship, creative activity, play, reading, research, and even thinking. You can program the electrodes so all the positive experiences of life are maximized, all the while you are in a tank like a blob of protoplasm. Would you want such a life, in which positive experiences are maximized? In which life is *full* of pleasure?

SOPHIA: Of course not.

SARAH: I don't know. Reminds me of a "Star Trek" episode.

PETER: Would we want a world in which people could constantly just hook themselves up to a pleasure machine, thereby maximizing "pleasures" in life?

SOPHIA: No.

SARAH: Maybe just on the weekends?

ANTHONY: Maybe drugs are pleasure machines.

PETER: What does this thought experiment show?

BOB: I believe it shows that what is valuable in life isn't just pleasure or experience, but the activities themselves.

SOPHIA: It's as if the stuff of life makes it worthwhile, actually living, *doing* these things, not just experiencing the pleasures. It's like the difference between going to a movie and living what the movie is about.

BOB: But a movie is at least a representation of life. Even that seems better than just the vicarious experience. In fact, life would be nothing but vicarious thrills.

PETER: So it appears that what is good in life, what makes us a concrete self whose life can be affected positively or negatively, is not just what happens *inside* us, as one philosopher says. The goods of life place us into a more substantial relation to the world we live in. We don't want to be a blob floating in a tank.

BOB: If utilitarianism wants to maximize happiness and minimize unhappiness in the world, how do you define happiness?

PETER: I don't think you can *define* "happiness" in the way you can define certain mathematical or scientific terms. But surely happiness involves living a life free from psychological or physical pain, enriched by significant companionship, friendship, relationships with others, enriched by creative and enjoyable employment, not worn down by tedious, nonfulfilling activities, with minimal boredom and a large variety of different kinds of experiences. There are simply many things that appear to constitute human happiness. Consequentialism, in its best form, should endorse the plurality of life's goods and recognize that judgments about the amount of good produced and the relative worth of certain goods will often be imprecise. I know that doesn't sound too helpful, but I think you'll see that any ethical theory must confront such ambiguities, sometimes because the ultimate principle involved is so vague you don't know how it applies, sometimes because there are a number of conflicting moral rules that seem to be involved, sometimes because a plurality of rights are claimed. Ethical theories don't take away all the difficulties of moral life.

ANTHONY: You mentioned moral rules and rights. Where are those in utilitarianism?

PETER: Let me answer by giving an example. Suppose I'm destitute, I have no job, I'm out of money, I have a very hungry family, I'm walking down a street, and I see a wallet. No one is around. I open it. It has one thousand dollars in it and it is owned by a local multimillionaire, owner of numerous factories and sweatshops renowned for their terrible working conditions, poor wages, and brutal labor tactics. I take the money out, leave the credit cards and personal items, and begin to walk away hurriedly. I stop. Ought I to take the money? *Morally*, is it right to keep the money, buy much-needed food and clothes for my children, and repair my car so I can seek out more job opportunities? What would you say? What would the consequentialist say?

ANTHONY: The consequentialist has to say it's okay to keep the money.

RANSOM: But it is stealing. That's not right. It's not his money. "Thou shalt not steal."

SOPHIA: Ah, but "love your neighbor," including your hungry children. That jerk won't miss the cash, and he may *deserve* to lose his money like that. Keep the cash, don't be sentimental, feed your children.

SARAH: There's "the end justifies the means" again. So stealing is okay for the utilitarian?

SOPHIA: Robin Hood lives!

PETER: Again, we don't want to simplify, but Anthony asked about the status of moral rules in utilitarianism, like the rule against stealing. It's another very sticky question associated with this moral theory. If the consequentialist holds that we must simply try to produce the best consequences, or maximize overall good, and we can do that by breaking some widely accepted moral rule, then we're permitted, . . . no, we're *required,* to break it. In this sense, there's something potentially radical about the doctrine. It can never be criticized for being "abstract" or ignoring the particular circumstances of situations. That might disturb some people.

RANSOM: I'm not sure I could accept that.

PETER: On the other hand, in most situations, widely accepted moral rules, like "don't steal," "tell the truth," and "don't kill," are relatively sound generalizations about the consequences of certain *types* of action. If we don't have time to calculate the consequences, if we are unsure, such moral rules are helpful "rules of thumb" for our actions, as philosophers say. In fact, being trained to act according to such rules has very positive consequences, socially, so acting according to them and teaching your children to abide by them are good things.

BOB: But in the crunch, if you're quite confident that more good can be done by breaking a widely accepted moral rule, then you ought to.

PETER: Yes, at least for so-called *act utilitarianism.* There is another version of utilitarianism that has a somewhat different interpretation of the status of moral rules. That's *rule utilitarianism.*

ANTHONY: Hold it. Before we talk about that, what about the issue of rights? What does utilitarianism say about rights?

PETER: What kind of rights?

ANTHONY: Human rights. To be free, to vote, to speak.

PETER: Actually, the father of utilitarianism, Jeremy Bentham, called the doctrine of natural rights "nonsense on stilts." Most consequentialists find such claims obscure; they feel it makes more sense to do away with these shadowy, abstract claims called rights. It's not that he felt that we should ignore the human goods associated with these so-called "rights." It's just that such claims are better placed in the context of a moral theory that talks about producing goodness for beings.

BOB: Not so fast. I see a big problem with utilitarianism, having to do with rights. Anthony mentioned affirmative action programs, and we know the controversy involved there. Then when we discussed my scholarship example, you said that utilitarianism always emphasizes overall good, even if it means that some people are shortchanged when others are very happy. If these things are true for utilitarianism, then isn't it possible that more overall good is produced when people are treated unfairly?

PETER: Can you give me an example?

ANTHONY: How about South Africa? It's a prosperous capitalist country—or it has been. But blacks are treated unfairly. It's grossly unjust to have a system of apartheid, even if you could somehow show that more happiness is produced for the minority.

PETER: You have to be careful here. You know what the consequentialist would say. He would say that the massive unhappiness caused by such an unjust system is *not* outweighed by prosperity experienced by the few. And this long-term social instability will continue as long as injustice occurs. He would say that it is precisely on consequentialist grounds that apartheid is to be judged as morally unacceptable.

BOB: But isn't it possible to have a social situation in which a small number of people are somehow enslaved and separated as the society functions better? And wouldn't that have to be accepted on utilitarian grounds?

SOPHIA: Why look at South Africa? Why not look in our own backyard? We have millions of homeless people, millions of people in poverty, millions with no health insurance. We have a permanent problem of structural unemployment. Yet we always hear that we're the richest, most prosperous country on earth. Aren't there people right here in America who pay for a system that promotes the most "overall happiness"?

ANTHONY: I have another situation that involves this issue. What about drug testing in the work place? Everyone jumps on the bandwagon because drugs sometimes cause problems, but I think it's a violation of my privacy to make me submit to a degrading test to see whether I might have used a relatively harmless recreational drug in my own home, privately.

RANSOM: But society can't tolerate the use of drugs, at home or anywhere else. It'll cause the downfall of our civilization if we continue like this. I'm really tired of all these privacy claims, when the very existence of society is threatened. Pornography, drugs, abortion. That's where we get these problems.

SOPHIA: I'm more interested in millions who are homeless than people who smoke pot in their homes.

RANSOM: Or do crack?

BOB: Is this relevant? Peter, restore some order.

PETER: Yes, it's quite relevant. I think many of these issues mentioned involve a tension between claims associated with producing overall social good and claims involving rights, or claims involving what seem to be nonconsequentialist or nonutilitarian moral values. Some philosophers have held that rights are the kind of moral claim that can't be overridden by appeals to maximizing good. Some of the examples point to the central objection raised by many against utilitarianism. It's often called the *justice objection*. The critics assert that there are at least *two* central features in morality: producing overall happiness and distributing it in a fair manner. Utilitarianism seems to sanction, at least in theory, unjust distributions of good. No one should be treated as a mere means for producing others' happiness. People should be treated fairly.

Notice, if I discriminate in distributing goodness solely on the basis of someone's color, I would be picking out a morally irrelevant characteristic of a person or group of persons. Race isn't relevant when people compete for jobs or for places in universities, try to buy houses, want to vote, etc.

BOB: So justice means that the majority can't use the minority to produce the most overall goods.

PETER: Yes, that's the central criticism. Another way it's been offered is to suggest that injustice might arise if you used a scapegoat of some kind to bring about social good. For example, it might be possible to punish an innocent person in order to quell some social unrest, and that would *seem* to be sanctioned on utilitarian grounds.

SOPHIA: You don't sound convinced.

PETER: I'm not. Many of these classic counterexamples seem to me to be impractical and farfetched. In the real world, police officials are found out if they convict innocent people on manufactured evidence and injustice causes social disruption and revolution. The long-term consequences of short-term violations of justice are *not* good. It still seems to me that on consequentialist grounds such speculative cases can be satisfactorily explained. There is, however, another route for the utilitarian to take. It seems to me a plausible way to preserve the spirit of consequentialism.

SOPHIA: One little problem before we move on?

PETER: Go ahead.

SOPHIA: Well, I almost didn't come on this trip. If I hadn't come, Rose wouldn't have either. I talked to the recreation office at the university and the policy is that at least six people are required in order for the trip to be sponsored. They can't afford a smaller number. This was the last trip of the summer and I knew that not only would I have been disappointed, so would several other people. The problem was that I had promised a friend I would officiate at her father's funeral. The father has been in a rest home for years in the southern part of the state but had broken his hip earlier in the summer and had not been doing well. My friend insisted that she could ask another minister and that it would not be a problem at all. I hadn't met the father or other members of the family. But I knew I would have to do it, even if my friend insisted that I should go on this trip. Well, the father did pass on five days before our trip started. I officiated at the funeral, so I didn't have to make a tough decision. But it occurs to me that if I had had to decide, I couldn't have come on the trip.

ROSE: You would have done the right thing.

SOPHIA: But I really didn't make any difference at the funeral. I didn't know the father. Few people attended the funeral. My friend could have gotten a better minister. I didn't do any good.

ROSE: Except to your friend.

SOPHIA: Yes, but I don't think she would have held it against me. But I felt that I had to keep my word, and that was more important than all of you disappointed people, and my own happiness. I wanted desperately to come on this trip. I felt I needed it. But I really never thought that overall happiness was most important. I felt that the promise was most important.

BOB: So if you had been a utilitarian, you would have come on the trip instead of keeping the promise. Very interesting. Let me add my own story. When my father died, I promised that I would use some of the money from the estate to establish a pet cemetery in his hometown. I thought it was a strange idea, but he loved pets and I promised. I *know* I could have done more good with that money, but I promised Dad. I did what he wanted.

SOPHIA: Yet there is the case of Franz Kafka, the great Czechoslovakian writer, who wanted his friend Max Brod to burn all of his manuscripts when he died. Suppose you were his friend and promised you would do this. Later, after Kafka dies, you realize that the world should not be deprived of Kafka's genius. Obviously, you shouldn't burn his writings. Fortunately, Max Brod agreed. Very puzzling.

BOB: The point remains. Sometimes a promise is more important than producing the most good.

PETER: Another excellent point. Not only does it seem that sometimes a promise is more important than producing overall happiness, as the examples show. Some have put it more strongly: The obligation to keep our promises is a nonutilitarian one. Sometimes when you are deciding what to do, you give no thought at all to producing the most good. You simply realize that you have made a promise and you must keep it. That's what a promise is.

SOPHIA: But sometimes we *do* break promises if we can produce more good. I might promise to meet you at noon to play tennis, but on the way I see a car wreck. I stop to help and break the appointment. That's the morally right thing to do. It produces more good.

PETER: Perhaps that simply shows that utilitarian obligations sometimes override nonutilitarian ones, not that utilitarian obligations are the *only* ones. But I still think the utilitarian could respond. He might say that your willingness to keep your promise and Bob's willingness to spend money on a pet cemetery are just the judgments of an ordinary or common morality. He is quite willing to repudiate these judgments, sometimes at least, precisely because the overall good is most important, morally speaking. Maybe we should reject the conservative sentimentalism of common morals.

BOB: I would have a very difficult time accepting that.

ALICE: I'm still not convinced that overall good and justice are compatible.

ANTHONY: Or that the greatest happiness won't conflict with individual rights.

SARAH: So now we've said that if you're a utilitarian you can steal, break promises, and violate rights? I've got to learn not to agree with things so easily. Sometimes things sound better than they are.

PETER: Again, I would caution against too easily accepting either the conclusions drawn from speculative examples where complications are ignored or the comfortable conclusions derived from common moral judgments. Because they're common doesn't mean they're right, and in speculative situations we have to consider people as they are, with complex expectations and desires. And, in any case, there is still another approach to utilitarianism that has attempted to respond to these criticisms.

ANTHONY: That's what you mentioned when I asked about moral rules.

PETER: Yes. *Rule Utilitarianism.* Briefly, it says that acts are morally right if they conform to rules that, if acted on generally, would maximize overall good.

SARAH: Come again?

PETER: Act utilitarianism says that for every act you should apply the test of utility directly; do what will bring about the best consequences, the most good. Rule utilitarianism thinks the most overall good is brought about by acting according to moral rules, so it uses the test of consequences more indirectly. An act is right if it is consistent with a correct moral rule. In turn, a moral rule is correct or acceptable if everyone's acting according to it will bring about the most overall good. There is no doubt that the rules requiring us to keep our promises and to tell the truth are extremely valuable socially. The act utilitarian says such rules are handy generalizations about the *types* of action that *usually* produce the best consequences, but they can be broken in specific situations when more good is produced. The rule utilitarian says that conformity with a valuable moral rule *makes* an act right. He says we should seek a system of rules that, if acted on by everyone, would produce the most happiness.

DONOVAN: And if the rules conflict, what are we to do? Eh, Professor? [Donovan walks out of the shadows and sits down by Sophia.] Another interesting night of philosophical chatter? Good evening, philosophers. [Donovan looks around the group and smiles.] Please don't let me stop the conversation.

SOPHIA: Peter? If the rules conflict? What do we do?

DONOVAN: Why, of course we do what will produce the most good, and now you're back to your old friend, the direct view, the extreme version, the *pure* version, the simple, no-frills brand, the obvious and useful *theory*, just produce the right consequences. We philosophers, we radicals, like the theory because it counteracts the stodgy moral conservatism of the absolutists. Especially the right-wingers. The act version can get you everything your ruling utilitarian rulers want. In *most* cases, don't think, don't count, just do it. Most of the sheep will do that. No problem. *But, but,* when you can get out your calculator, do it, by all means! Right, Peter?

PETER: As my students would say, you're really too much, my friend. Perhaps *you're* oversimplifying this time.

DONOVAN: Am I? Suppose you have your system of rules and you must wonder which are most important in specific cases. The most important rules in cases of conflict or even throughout the system, are those that maximize overall good. Aren't they?

PETER: So Donovan is saying that the rule version reduces itself to using directly the principle of producing the best consequences in specific situations, for every act.

DONOVAN: Tell the truth. Very important. But don't hurt another person. As long as you know you *can* produce the "greatest happiness," you have to, if you're a utilitarian magician.

PETER: All right, Donovan. I'll waive the objections. You know the moves a rule utilitarian might make. Let's press the point. Let's stick to the "extreme" version of consequentialism. You're right to emphasize the fact that many thinkers are sympathetic to it because they can't accept a kind of unthinking idolatry of abstract, quite general rules, written in heaven or elsewhere. I admit that I'm sympathetic to consequentialism, but not as the final word.

DONOVAN: Which word do we take it to be?

PETER: We take it to be a profound expression of the impartiality demanded by morality, which must be included in our moral reflections.

DONOVAN: You've said the magic word. *Demanding.* Demanding? Let me count the ways. [Donovan turns to the rest of the group.] I want you to think carefully about what your life would be like if you accepted such consequentialism. Your job in life, morally speaking, is quite clear: Produce as much good as you can whenever you act. What *are* you, as a self? You're a resource, whose constant moral job is the production of good. There's no time for play, you moral workaholic. Are you doing all you can in life to make the world better? Should you be here at all? Isn't this backpacking trip self-indulgent? You could spend these days working in soup kitchens, helping adults to read, gathering food for the poor in your community. Some of you, no doubt, are prosperous. Do you give all you can to charity? Of course, for the utilitarian, it's not charity at all. It's your *duty* to give, to a point where it will begin to affect you and your family negatively. Have you given up all the luxuries of life? You could contribute to world hunger funds. Have Peter explain the difference between obligations and *supererogation.*

PETER: Obligation describes those acts we think we are morally *required* to perform. Supererogatory acts are those we believe are *beyond duty*, but are morally praiseworthy. Donovan is arguing that consequentialism is too demanding because it transforms acts that *he* thinks are supererogatory into ones that we are required to perform—like giving money to charity or making great sacrifices for others.

SARAH: Like someone falling on a grenade in war, to save others.

RANSOM: Or attempting to save someone from a burning house.

DONOVAN: Even in your system of rules, wouldn't there have to be rules requiring such actions, so good will be maximized?

PETER: Perhaps not, since people will simply ignore so-called moral rules that require great personal sacrifice.

DONOVAN: Consider a friend of mine, one of the most talented ladies I've ever met. We were students together as undergraduates. She was the most accomplished artist in school, a wonderful painter, she loved literature and was coveted by the literature professors, she was the best philosophy major as a senior, *but* . . . her father is a physician, a fine and generous man, and a profound influence on her. She took the basic science courses required for medical school, aced the MCAT, and then had to decide what to do with her life. Artist? Graduate school in English? Philosophy? Or physician? A difficult, difficult choice. But not if you're a utilitarian. Ignore the other talents. The self is merely a permanent possibility for producing goodness, not a concrete, highly specific being with certain talents, capabilities, projects, commitments, and *personal* urgencies. Artists and philosophers can't contribute to overall happiness as a physician can. For the consequentialist, there's no dilemma—and no self.

PETER: I daresay that I shouldn't be surprised if she did decide to go to medical school, because she realized that she could do more good for the world by becoming a physician. Perhaps her own happiness need not have suffered.

DONOVAN: The issue was whether this is obviously *required*, morally. Where do we stake out our private claims in such a morality? Do you recall J. L. Mackie's wonderful description of act utilitarianism? He called it the "ethics of fantasy," because it is so very impractical. We can't live like this. It leaves us no self to be, other than someone devoted to our constant moral chores. After all, there's much to be done.

RANSOM: But if Mill thought it was what Jesus meant by telling us to "love your neighbor as yourself," you're just saying that we don't want to take Jesus' teachings seriously.

DONOVAN: Just another version of the ethics of fantasy, as Mackie also said. I'm saying we *can't* take such an ethic seriously. We're too interested in our own lives, as we should be.

SOPHIA: Back to egoism?

DONOVAN: Let me give you one last example to think about. It's a variation of a famous example that Peter is well aware of, but it happened. Another friend of mine went to graduate school in biology at a very prestigious school that had the number one program in his area of research interest. When he got there, he found that the professor he was to work with, the most highly respected person in the field, was using chimps and other animals in the most cruel and despicable ways you can imagine. Now my friend, let's call him Tom, was the most vocal and committed animal rights activist I knew, or have known—except for Peter here. This caused him a severe conflict. The professor thought that the notion of animal rights was silly. If Tom stayed, he might be able to do something for the welfare of the animals, but the professor would not stop the research nor the use of animals. If Tom left the program, the professor could get someone else, probably this time screened for softness on the animal rights issue. The professor also despised animal rights activists and told Tom that if Tom left the program he would make it difficult for him to get into any other top program or to publish any research in the area. (The professor edited the main journal in the area.) So what would produce the most good? What should he do? If he didn't help the professor, some other, more insensitive, graduate student would. Tom's career was at issue. Tom *might* be able to help the animals. *And*, Tom had recently married and his wife was expecting their first child. Life is sometimes difficult, isn't it?

SOPHIA: I know what I would do . . . I think. I couldn't go ahead with the research. I just couldn't.

DONOVAN: Yet consequentialism seems to indicate that there is really no difficulty here. *Obviously*, Tom should take the fellowship and help with the professor's research. What difference would it really make if he left, other than make his own life more difficult. But Tom didn't stay, because he has *integrity*. He remained committed to his values, to his personal commitments. He didn't believe that *he* could participate in research tainted by animal suffering, although, if he had, perhaps more "total good" would have been produced. A dilemma, Peter? What are we to do with our private commitments in such a moral scheme?

SOPHIA: If they are *too* private, if they ignore or violate others' interests, aren't we back to the egoist's ballpark?

DONOVAN: You see, I'm out here in the mountains, hurting no one, but I'm certainly not helping others as much as I could. It's not only the outright possible harm to a few that is morally problematic for consequentialism. You've talked about justice, no doubt. It's also the doctrine that my *not* doing things also has consequences, and I'm as responsible for the consequences arising from my omissions as from my commissions, my positive acts. But to live a full life, and to be committed to my personal vision of what I want my life to be, I simply can't see my own commitments as impersonally equal to everyone else's.

SOPHIA: But Donovan, you must admit that consequentialism insists that we must *care* for others, for everyone. Caring is important.

DONOVAN: To a fault? Such that I must give up my life because the deity people call "morality" forces me to be a moral fanatic? There are other routes to the moral life. Don't feel coerced or guilty if you're not a moral saint. It's not an ideal I find inviting.

RANSOM: But we can be more like Jesus.

DONOVAN: Of course, we *can*. That's not the point.

BOB: What is the point?

DONOVAN: [He pauses, smiles.] I have no idea. Do you Peter?

PETER: Don't try to be ironic; it's unbecoming. You can be more helpful than that.

DONOVAN: Let's just say that I prefer to see the self as a chooser, as a free agent, whose life we need to *respect*, who must ask what he is to *be* in this dance we call life. Is that better? [He leaps to his feet and jumps into the air.] I, for one, love being on the soil! In these mountains! You people chatter too much! You should be drinking and dancing! I'll help this party. You're going across the pass, to Lost Lake?

RANSOM: Yes. We'll be there for a few days.

DONOVAN: Wonderful! I'll teach you to dance—and to fish! Good night. [He walks away.]

What Thinkers Have Said

. . . *The creed which accepts as the foundation of morals, Utility, or the Greatest Happiness Principle, holds that actions are right in proportion as they tend to promote happiness, wrong as they tend to produce the reverse of happiness. By happiness is intended pleasure, and the absence of pain; by unhappiness, pain, and the privation of pleasure. To give a clear view of the moral standard set up by the theory, much more requires to be said; in particular, what things it includes in the ideas of pain and pleasure; and to what extent this is left an open question. But these supplementary explanations do not affect the theory of life on which this theory of morality is grounded—namely, that pleasure, and freedom from pain, are the only things desirable as ends; and that all desirable things (which are as numerous in the utilitarian as in any other scheme) are desirable either for the pleasure inherent in themselves, or as means to the promotion of pleasure and the prevention of pain.*

John Stuart Mill, *Utilitarianism*

It is better to be a human being dissatisfied than a pig satisfied; better to be Socrates dissatisfied than a fool satisfied. And if the fool, or the pig, are of a different opinion, it is because they only know their own side of the question. The other party to the comparison knows both sides.

John Stuart Mill, *Utilitarianism*

. . . *The question of whether the "higher" pleasures should be preferred to the "lower" ones does seem to be of slight practical importance. There are already perfectly good hedonistic arguments for poetry as against pushpin. As has been pointed out, the more complex pleasures are incomparably more fecund that the less complex ones: not only are they enjoyable in themselves but they are a means to further enjoyment. Still less, on the whole, do they lead to disillusionment, physical deterioration or social disharmony. The connoisseur of poetry may enjoy himself no more than the connoisseur of whisky, but he runs no danger of a headache on the following morning. Moreover the question of whether the general happiness would be increased by replacing most of the human population by a bigger population of contented sheep and pigs is not one which by any stretch of the imagination could become a live issue. Even if we thought, on abstract grounds, that such a replacement would be desirable, we should have the slightest chance of having our ideas generally adopted . . .*

J. J. C. Smart, "An Outline of a System of Utilitarian Ethics"

Utilitarian thinking has practical importance (assuming that it is adopted) in so far as it differs from common sense and traditional moral thinking. An important respect in which this is so is that utilitarianism leaves no room for ordinary moral notions of justice and of rights. This does not mean, however, that a utilitarian may not support legal and customary rules of justice and of right. He or she may hold that such rules, enforceable either legally or by pressure of public opinion, may be extremely useful.

J. J. C. Smart, "Utilitarianism and Its Applications"

Given the comprehensiveness, plausibility, and overall rationality of consequentialism, it is not unreasonable to override even a deeply felt moral conviction if it does not square with such a theory, though, if it made no sense or overrode the bulk of or even a great many of our considered moral convictions, that would be another matter indeed.

Kai Nielsen, "Against Moral Conservatism"

Key Terms and Concepts

utilitarianism

ends justify the means

greatest happiness of the greatest number of people

predicting consequences

aggregate good

hedonism

quantity of pleasure vs. quality of pleasure

experience machine

defining happiness

act utilitarianism vs. rule utilitarianism

justice objection

promising

supererogation

"ethics of fantasy"

integrity

Questions

1. How is utilitarianism correctly formulated? Why is the popular formulation ("greatest happiness of the greatest number") ambiguous?

2. Can we adequately predict the consequences of our actions? Is this a difficult problem for utilitarianism?

3. Explain why the thought experiment concerning the so-called "experience machine" undermines hedonism.

4. Is utilitarianism a "radical" moral doctrine? Does it conflict with conventional morality?

5. What is the justice objection to utilitarianism? What are the long-term consequences of significant injustice in a social situation?

6. Some philosophers have associated act utilitarianism with so-called "situation ethics." Is this accurate? Is this a strength or a weakness?

7. Does act utilitarianism ignore the significance of our commitment to moral rules in decision making and moral education?

8. Try to formulate a definition of moral rightness according to rule utilitarianism. Reflect on the genesis of moral rules for the rule utilitarian.

9. Explain the difference between obligation and supererogation. Is utilitarianism too demanding?

10. Some philosophers have attempted to define the notion of a moral saint by relating it to supererogation. Do you think this is a satisfactory way to clarify moral sainthood?

11. Do you think utilitarianism fails to explain satisfactorily the value we place on personal integrity?

12. Do you think some moral theories expect too much from moral agents?

Suggested Readings

Bayles, Michael, D., ed, *Contemporary Utilitarianism*, Anchor Books, 1968. Excellent collection of articles both supporting and critizing utilitarianism.

Bentham, Jeremy, *Introduction to the Principles of Morals and Legislation*, W. Harrison, ed., Oxford, 1948. Seminal presentation of the utilitarian position. Also contains an interesting defense of "quantitative" hedonism.

Brandt, Richard, "Toward a Credible Form of Rule Utilitarianism," in *Morality and the Language of Conduct*, H. N. Castaneda and George Nakhnikian, eds; Wayne State, 1963. Occurs commonly in anthologies. Argues that rule utilitarianism is in principle a satisfactory moral theory.

Mackie, J. L., *Ethics: Inventing Right and Wrong*, Penguin, 1976. Characterizes act utilitarianism as an "ethics of fantasy."

Mill, John Stuart, *Utilitarianism*, London, 1861. Classic presentation of the utilitarian's position, with important modifications of Bentham's view. Contains a defense of "qualitative" hedonism.

Nielsen, Kai, "Against Moral Conservatism," *Ethics*, 82, 1972.

Nozick, Robert, *Anarchy, State and Utopia*, Basic Books, 1974. Describes the "experience machine" in order to criticize hedonism.

Rachels, James, *The Elements of Moral Philosophy*, chs. 7 and 8, Random House, 1986. Summary of standard arguments for and against utilitarianism.

Smart, J. J. C. and William, Bernard, *Utilitarianism: For and Against*, Cambridge, 1973. "An Outline of a System of Utilitarian Ethics," by Smart is a lucid defense of utilitarianism. "A Critique of Utilitarianism" by Williams discusses the problem of integrity for utilitarianism.

Dialogue Six:
Ethics and Persons

In this dialogue, the ethical theory inspired by the great German philosopher Immanuel Kant is discussed. Rose's initial comments about the "absolute" character of morality provoke a lively interchange concerning universal moral rules and respect for the unconditional value of persons. The dialogue ends with Sophia questioning whether a viewpoint emphasizing respect for persons might lead to an attitude of indifference when we are faced with situations in which we might help people.

ROSE: Peter, I know I'm no philosopher, and I don't think I've understood even half of what we've talked about . . .

SOPHIA: You always underestimate yourself. [To the others.] This is a lady who could have done anything in life.

ROSE: Oh, I doubt that. But these conversations are the first time I've ever thought about some of these things. I can't believe everything we've talked about. The last conversation, though, was disturbing. I never took the ideas about selfishness too seriously. I'm sorry, Mark. I know there are selfish people in life; I just thought their parents didn't teach them how to be good people. Last night was different.

PETER: How so?

ROSE: I wanted to believe we had finally gotten to the best ethical view, that we should care for others and do what we're supposed to do. But we ended up in a confusing place. If you're a consequentialist you can justify *anything*, if you just say you're trying to promote happiness.

PETER: I would still insist that it's not quite that simple, but I understand your concern.

ROSE: Then your friend Donovan had some interesting things to say, although I'm not sure where he's coming from. It's just that . . . well . . . what's all this theorizing about? I don't understand it. It's as if we're trying to talk ourselves out of thinking that we should be caring and we should do some things that we know are right. We *know* we have to do certain things. I couldn't keep someone's money, I couldn't lie to someone, I couldn't break my word, no matter what. Some things can never be done just for the sake of consequences.

SOPHIA: But Rose, can't you think of *any* situation in which you might have to do one of these things?

ROSE: How are we supposed to teach our children? Do we tell them it's okay to lie as long as you can justify it to your conscience? That you can do it whenever you want?

BOB: Rose, I'm sympathetic to what you're saying, but we have to be fair to the other position. Perhaps we have to be absolutists when we teach our children, until they have enough good judgment to realize that on rare occasions we can break absolute rules if something more important comes up.

ALICE: Then they're not absolute. It's the "more important"; that's the problem. It does seem too easy to say, "Well, I'll do this since more good can be done if I do it."

ANTHONY: I have a feeling that the biggest problem is the other way around.

ALICE: What do you mean?

ANTHONY: Well, I think you should be very certain that more happiness would be produced if you're going to break some moral rule like promising or stealing.

ALICE: Or killing? Or kidnapping?

ANTHONY: I don't know. I think there are certain times when it's all right to break the rules that some people think are "absolute." You've got to be certain about the consequences, though. But the other problem is that sometimes people do things that are wrong and then they say it was okay because it didn't cause any harm to anybody else.

PETER: Very interesting. We wondered last night whether there were situations in which moral values other than consequences were crucial for deciding what to do. You have touched on a very interesting way to see how an appeal to nonconsequentialist values or principles is often important. What do you have in mind?

ANTHONY: You seem to be a step ahead of me.

PETER: I confess that I do have something in mind, but you tell us what you're thinking about.

ANTHONY: It's my next door neighbor. When Mark told us about his friend, I couldn't help thinking of George. I've lived next to him for years. Here's the kind of guy he is. It's been a few years, but it's still crystal clear in my mind. I'm gassing up at a filling station, putting unleaded gas in my little car and George drives up. He's got a big car and he starts filling up with *regular* gas. He just smiles at me. I ask him what's going on. He says he knocked out the filler tank and took off the catalytic converter. Didn't want to pay extra for the gas. When I asked about the pollution, he said, "Hey, I ain't hurtin' nobody. You think my car makes any difference? I can't afford the gas anyway."

PETER: And what did you say? Did you try to convince him that he shouldn't have done it?

ANTHONY: I asked him, "What if everyone did that?"

SOPHIA: And?

ANTHONY: He just said something like "Not everyone will do it." He said he wasn't like everyone else. This is a guy who throws cigarettes and beer cans out of his car window, cheats like crazy on his taxes, and . . . get this. Every time he sells his car, he rolls back the odometer at least fifteen thousand miles so he can get more on the trade-in.

SOPHIA: This is a friend?

ANTHONY: He's not a bad guy. I can't say he's socially responsible, but he always says he's not hurting anyone. He doesn't think he's a bad guy.

PETER: So he insists that the consequences of his actions aren't negative, since the effects of his actions are minimal when seen from the larger, social perspective, and *he* experiences certain benefits from them.

SOPHIA: He just sounds like another egoist.

PETER: But what is interesting is that it is at least plausible to consider that he *is* correct in some cases, that the consequences of his actions are socially minimal and they have positive effects for him and his family. But Anthony is still bothered by such behavior.

SOPHIA: I am, too.

ALICE: Really, he's a jerk. Why bother?

ANTHONY: No, he's not. He's been a good friend.

ALICE: To whom? Not to the person who ends up buying his used car.

ANTHONY: I don't think he really thinks he is doing anything wrong.

ALICE: Rolling back the odometer? That's deceptive. He's using people.

PETER: Let's push this. What about the original example? What, exactly, is Anthony's criticism? What if everyone did that? What is he saying?

SARAH: His friend is right. Who is it? George? George says that not everyone will do what he does, so the consequences aren't really that bad.

ALICE: But if some people do these things, so will others. And if everyone did them, the consequences *would* be disastrous. Why do you think we have pollution devices anyway?

ANTHONY: But how many people are going to find out that George did it?

PETER: And, of course, he could keep his action secret, or at least as secret as possible. In that case, there's no reason to think his actions will cause others to do likewise. But that's still not really the crux of Anthony's original criticism, is it?

SARAH: The consequences of everyone doing it are bad, but not many people will take off their catalytic converters. Isn't there a law against it?

PETER: So what is the criticism? Doesn't it have a great deal to do with a moral principle we've heard? And used?

SARAH: Like?

PETER: Anthony asks, "What if everyone did that?" He wants George to recognize that *George* wouldn't like it if everyone were to do what he happens to be doing.

SARAH: You mean "Do unto others as you would have them do unto you"?

PETER: Precisely. Isn't the force of the moral criticism that George is acting in a certain way and he wouldn't want others to act that way?

ANTHONY: Sure. And if he wouldn't want others to act that way, then he shouldn't act that way. It's as if we're saying, "Who do you think you are?"

PETER: So what, precisely, is the basis for the wrongness in this situation?

SOPHIA: Doesn't it involve the issue of impartiality or equality? Isn't that something you harped on earlier, Peter? That's just another way of saying that we all have the same status.

BOB: It's a matter of consistency. Here's a person who is inconsistent. He wants to do something that he wouldn't want others to do.

SARAH: But not everybody is the same. I don't expect others to be like me.

PETER: However, morally, it's just this sense that I *am* like everybody else that is central to our moral directives, isn't it? And here's another way of getting at it, this time from a nonconsequentialist perspective.

BOB: You'd better say more about this.

PETER: This part of our moral thinking was emphasized by the eighteenth-century German philosopher Immanuel Kant. He is a very difficult thinker, and many of his views are rooted in a very complex systematic approach to philosophy. However, he certainly thought he was offering a reconstruction of the common moral consciousness of his time. For him, the essence of doing the right thing was acting strictly according to duty, wanting to do something not because it will help you achieve your *own* goals or help you advance any goals you might have, but simply acting because you want to do the right thing, period. Now for Kant, duty was essentially related to acting from respect for law. He conceived of moral rules as absolutely binding moral laws. There's Rose's sense of the absolute character of morality. For him, *the* supreme principle in morality is that we should act according to absolute moral rules. This squares with our intuition that some things can *never* be done for the sake of consequences, as Rose suggested.

SARAH: What kind of absolute rules?

PETER: Like the moral rule that we should tell the truth. Or keep our promises. For Kant, the central characteristic of a law is that it extends to everyone equally; that is, it is universal. So he felt that acting on the basis of moral rules that could be made universal would be tantamount to doing one's duty. If you can't universalize the rule you are acting on, then you are acting according to a directive that couldn't be a law, hence you wouldn't be acting strictly from duty.

ROSE: Peter, you're losing me. What does this have to with Anthony's example?

PETER: It's this, I think. If moral laws or rules are universal, they apply to everyone equally. That means that I can't make myself an arbitrary exception to moral requirements. George wanted to do something he expected others not to do. But what if we tried to make a *universally binding* moral rule out of what is assumed by his action? What rule describes his action?

ANTHONY: It's okay to take off a pollution-control device . . .

PETER: But?

ANTHONY: But it's not okay for others to do it.

PETER: Or "I can take off the pollution-control device but others cannot." What happens when I try to "universalize" this so it applies to everyone?

BOB: I see! Ingenious. It can't be done. You want to be an exception to the rule, but if it applies to everyone, then *everyone* is an exception. But that means no one is an exception. Universal application is impossible.

PETER: On straightforward logical grounds. There's something self-defeating about such a rule when universalized. It's logically problematic when it applies to everyone. Kant seemed to think he had discovered a quite practical method to show us what our duties are.

SOPHIA: Does it show us what our duties are, or what they're not? Anthony's example shows us what's morally wrong to do. It shows that if we do something we don't want others to do, then our arbitrariness is wrong. I'm not sure I understand this.

PETER: Superb question. There are all kinds of knotty problems associated with this part of Kant's moral thinking, but he seems to have a keen point. We can't be arbitrary. Morality binds us to other beings, and there is a kind of logic embedded in our moral judgments, a logic that says that what applies to you also applies to me. This logic comes out best when it appears to be violated by people like George. Kant's test of universalizability—that's quite a mouthful—shows this. It also works when we think of the duty to keep our promises, or not to break contractual relationships. For example, suppose I make a promise with no intention to keep it, perhaps to get me out of some difficult situation. What's my assumed moral rule? What happens when it is universalized?

Bob: I can make a lying promise, or when universalized, everyone can make a lying promise.

Peter: Problem?

Sophia: If everyone could be lying when a promise is made, then no one would believe a promise.

Peter: In other words, there could be no promises in such a situation. Again, when universalized, there is something self-defeating about such a moral rule.

Sophia: But, obviously, sometimes it is all right to break a promise. We've gone through this before. Did Kant believe that we could never, *ever* break a promise?

Peter: Evidently he did. We have absolutely binding obligations never to lie and to keep our promises. Let me go back to your original question. Many philosophers have felt that Kant was right to insist that moral rules are somehow universal, so if a rule can't be universal, there's something suspicious about it. On the other hand, even if a rule can be made universal, it may not follow that it is right. As an example to think about, consider the first principle of egoism: Everyone should attempt to maximize his self-interest. We *could* all act according to this, couldn't we? I see nothing self-defeating about it. But I don't find it an acceptable ultimate moral principle. One of Kant's own examples is particularly telling in this respect. He thought that we have a duty to help others when they need it, since we may sometimes need the help of others, and we would be inconsistent if we expected others to help us at some time but we never helped them. But what if, when I needed the help of others, I don't expect to be helped? I would be consistent then.

Sophia: That's the big problem of "Do unto others." If all you're required to do is to be consistent, then you could be a consistent individualist, never helping others and expecting no help in return.

Peter: Yes.

Sophia: And you still have the other problem. Sometimes it's acceptable to lie, for example. Or to break a promise. Sometimes there are more important things to consider, and not necessarily selfish ones. Suppose I promised to meet someone and then my mother has a heart attack. I rush her to the hospital and break my promise. That's not wrong.

PETER: Apply Kant's test. What's the moral rule? Is it universalizable?

SOPHIA: Let's see . . . If I or anyone has made a promise but I can help to save someone's life by breaking it, it's morally right to do so. I don't see why that can't be a moral rule for everyone. We would still believe others' promises most of the time.

PETER: I agree. This is one of the great problems of Kant's ethical views. He had such a stringent sense of absolute duty as essential to morality that he was not able to account for legitimate exceptions to moral rules. And, when he talked about the supposed moral rule at issue in his examples, he always talked in the most general terms. It does seem, however, that we could describe moral rules more situationally and the results of universalization would be quite different. He doesn't really explain how to decide what the relevant moral rule is. Sometimes an action can be described as, for example, a violation of promise keeping *in* a certain situation.

ROSE: Now we're back to situational ethics. I still have this sense that we're being too theoretical and we're trying to make it too easy to avoid doing what we know is right.

PETER: Notice another very difficult problem for Kant, arising from the particular circumstances of some situations. What if I face a conflict between two supposedly absolute duties? I might have promised someone I would protect a confidence and then I might be faced with having to lie to keep my promise. But if both promise keeping and truth telling are "absolute" duties, I'm in an impossible situation.

SOPHIA: There's something else, too. What about Donovan's comments last night? I really liked some of that. Utilitarianism says that everyone's good is to be counted the same. There's the equality. Now Kant says that the moral rules I act on must apply to everyone and I can't make myself an exception. I accept that in some situations, such as the case of Anthony's friend, George. But I *am* a unique self. I can act in ways that I wouldn't expect of others. Not everyone can be a Unitarian minister, or have my beliefs and interests. How do we tell when it is morally acceptable to do things that couldn't work for everyone? Kant may rule out arbitrariness, but doesn't he also rule out being a legitimate exception? Not everyone can be a philosopher, a priest, a lawyer, or a tennis player.

PETER: Perhaps we can answer your question and respond to Rose's sense of the absolute character of moral requirements by considering another part of Kant's moral philosophy. I must say that this is the aspect of Kant's thinking that has probably been most important for a great many people, especially recently for philosophers doing work in applied ethics. Do you recall what Alice said a few minutes ago about George rolling back the odometer?

ALICE: I said it's deceptive.

PETER: And?

ALICE: That George *uses* people, which he does.

PETER: How so?

ALICE: My husband doesn't want to hear this, but George does use people. The pollution aspect is just an example. Even there I think he's manipulating others for his own interests. It's like the whole world is there for George to use for his own purposes, and he gives nothing back in return.

ANTHONY: That's not right. That's not George.

ALICE: When's the last time he did something for you? You're just too nice to say no to him. Have you ever talked to people who have worked for him? He treats them like they're just a piece of business equipment.

ANTHONY: Hey, in business you can't always be "Mr. Nice Guy."

ALICE: But you can be a *human* being, can't you? And treat others like humans, too.

PETER: Instead of . . . ?

ALICE: Instead of just something else he needs for his business, to be thrown away like a piece of garbage.

PETER: Let's think about this. You say that George's behavior is symptomatic of his failure to treat people properly, that he uses people, treats them as things rather than persons.

ALICE: That's right.

PETER: You assume, of course, as Kant himself did, that there is something fundamentally distinct about a person as opposed to a thing. Kant made this point a central feature of his ethics. He argued that we should always treat humanity, what is central to our personhood, in ourselves as well as others, as an *end in itself,* and *never merely as a means.* People sometimes call this principle Kant's *respect for persons* formulation of his ultimate ethical principle. He thought he was simply giving another way of understanding the notion that we ought to act on the basis of universal, absolute moral rules.

BOB: How's that?

PETER: Perhaps we can understand this by considering why he stressed, as Alice has, the difference between persons and things. What is the difference?

SARAH: Hold it. I don't understand the stuff about ends and means. What does that mean?

PETER: We are to treat people as ends and not *merely* as means. What would it be like to treat somebody merely as a means? Give me an example of treating something as a means.

SARAH: Means to what?

BOB: To some end or purpose or goal I might have. For example, we're sitting on a log. We're using the log as a means, aren't we? We're sitting on it. We're using it for our purposes.

PETER: Using that example, what would it be like to use a person merely as a means?

BOB: I suppose if I asked someone to be my log! If I used someone so I could sit on him to keep my backside from getting damp, and to be more comfortable. That would be treating someone as a means.

SARAH: That's silly. No one is going to use someone else like that. No one would stand for it.

SOPHIA: But that's the point Peter is helping us to see. We do sometimes treat people as if they were things, not real, sensitive, thinking beings. We shouldn't treat them as if they were just there for our own purposes. We may not treat people as pieces of furniture, but people do use others. They use others as sexual objects, for example.

MARK: But we have to use others, in a sense. We do it all the time. I go to a mechanic to help me fix my car, so I use him for my purposes. We're using Ransom and Sarah to help us on this trip. We use people when we go to the store, when we see the doctor, or even the *lawyer*.

PETER: That's why Kant's principle says we can't treat people *merely* as means. We must respect them, and not treat them as if they were a *mere* thing, useful only for our purposes. This doesn't absolutely rule out using people to help us.

SARAH: What's the difference?

SOPHIA: There's a huge difference between using a mechanic and, for example, using someone as a slave. You can respect a mechanic by being friendly or not being rude. If you enslave someone, you deny the person's freedom and dignity. You treat a person as a *mere* thing, an object to use only for your own purposes.

PETER: So what is the difference between a person and a thing, in terms of what you have called dignity? Think of it in terms of value, or at least estimating the value of a thing as opposed to a person.

ROSE: I sometimes think of this when I hear the term "unwanted child." Whether a child is unwanted or not, it's so very precious.

PETER: Why do *things* have value?

BOB: A piece of furniture has value because people want to be comfortable when they sit down. They also like to look at attractive furniture.

PETER: And if a piece of furniture is "unwanted," what value does it have?

BOB: None, as far as I can see. No one would buy it or use it.

PETER: A child? What value does it have? What does such value depend on?

SOPHIA: A child's value doesn't depend on anyone. You can't calculate the value of a child or a person.

PETER: There is the Kantian point. I've heard a rather nice way of putting this. A person is to his dignity as a thing is to its price, in terms of estimating its value or worth. A thing has what Kant called conditional worth. Its price, if we think in monetary terms, is *relative* to or conditioned by people bestowing value on it because of their needs or interests or desires. So conditional worth is imposed by something *external* to the thing. The dignity of a person is quite different. A person has unconditional worth. As Sophia said, we can't estimate the value of a person. It is *absolute*, not relative. Some speak of the infinite worth of persons. Such value is *intrinsic* to the person, not dependent on any external source. In short, Kant believed, quite rightly some think, that persons belong to a wholly different category of beings than things, in terms of their worth or value.

SOPHIA: So if you treat a person as a thing, you deny the person's dignity; you treat her as if she has value only if you happen to find her useful.

PETER: Yes. Here's Rose's sense of the absolute character of morality and also the answer to why Kant believed that acting on universal moral rules can be seen as treating people as ends in themselves. Notice that if Kant is right, moral rules apply to everyone without exception. Why? Because we are all equal. But why are we equal? Because we're all immeasurably valuable. This is the way we must look at ourselves and, to be consistent, at others. And,

Rose, you insist that there are some things that can never be done for the sake of consequences. The nonconsequentialist can sustain this insight by insisting that we must always respect the dignity, that is, the infinite value of persons, by insisting that persons not be treated as things to be used by others.

BOB: Even if more good, even great good, can be produced by doing so? The consequentialist says we can do whatever will bring about the best consequences, even if that means enslaving a minority or punishing an innocent person. Kant disagrees, I take it.

PETER: Yes. You cannot use a person as a mere thing or useful tool for promoting the most good. Kant's respect for persons principle is a solid basis for showing that such treatment is morally unacceptable. We would say that it's not *fair* or *just* to use people in this way.

SOPHIA: I assume that your answer to my question about when we can act in ways we wouldn't expect others to act would use this principle. I'm not using people in a morally bad way by being a Unitarian minister. Plantation owners *are* using people.

BOB: I like this principle. I think Kant is right to stress the fact that we must respect the unconditional worth of persons. But I'm still a little uncertain about what it means.

SOPHIA: Is it that you don't see how it applies?

BOB: I can see that you can't make slaves of people. But there are tougher problems. I'm a businessman. I've had to fire people for the good of the company. I know this has caused hardship. Is this a lack of respect? Have I simply treated them as things that are useful for my business? Or when I go to my office in a grumpy mood and hardly acknowledge the existence of my secretary, am I treating her as a thing rather than a person?

SOPHIA: Are you answering your own questions? Look, the first thing I think of when I think of people using other people has to do with women's issues. In our society, women are often treated as sexual objects, as things, not persons. It happens in ordinary relationships, it happens in prostitution, it happens in pornography, and now it even happens when women are turned into impersonal baby machines. Look at the difference between seeing these things as a consequentialist might see them and seeing them from Kant's perspective. Women are exploited in the bedroom, in the work place, in the entertainment industry . . . just look around.

MARK: But don't females often *choose* to be "exploited," as you say? No one is forced to be a prostitute. No one is forced to be in a pornographic movie.

SOPHIA: That's simply not true, in some cases. And in all situations we have to be aware of the social forces that drive people to do what they do, the enormous pressures on people to live in a society like ours.

MARK: Oh, come on, Sophia. You act like there are no alternatives for women.

SOPHIA: And other minorities? I sometimes wonder whether our society recognizes that it systematically robs people of their dignity when they are forced to do these things to survive.

BOB: See? This whole notion of respecting persons *is* unclear. We know we can't exploit people in certain ways, but do we also have to respect them if they *choose* to be exploited?

PETER: I think this may be clearer if we ask ourselves why we value persons so highly. In other words, what is it about a person that makes him or her so different from a thing, or even an animal? What is dignity based on?

MARK: It seems to me that it's based on the fact that we can choose. We're free and responsible beings.

PETER: For example, would you say that an animal makes choices, in your sense?

MARK: No.

PETER: Why not?

MARK: Because an animal acts on instinct. It can't think. It's unable to reflect on alternatives.

PETER: Actually, some people now think that as least *some* animals can choose, in your sense, but let's suppose that persons, at least, can do as you say. Why do people choose one alternative as opposed to another? In particular, think in terms of all these discussions about the moral dimension of human existence.

BOB: They have reasons.

PETER: What kind of reasons? Again, think of our discussions.

SOPHIA: Some reasons are selfish or self-interested, when we want things for ourselves. But sometimes we do things for moral reasons. That's what you're getting at, I suppose.

PETER: Yes. The Kantian tradition stresses the fact that we can act on the basis of moral reasons, that is, we can attempt to do our duty, or do what we think is right. We're responsible for our actions. We're *moral agents* who must determine for ourselves what to do in life.

MARK: We have to *choose*.

PETER: Yes. As self-determining agents, we are *autonomous*. Many philosophers make this notion the central feature of their ethical thinking. Respecting persons as rational, self-determining moral agents means that we must respect the autonomy of a person. You might say that this is the basis for holding that people have a right to make their own choices. Another way of putting it is that respect for another means that we must take the greatest care to guard the liberty of individuals. We must respect the judgments they make about their lives.

BOB: Unless they fail to respect the autonomy of others.

PETER: Yes.

BOB: But take the pornography issue. I detest this filth, but do I have to say it's acceptable if people choose to participate in it, look at it, read it? What would a follower of Kant say?

MARK: Legally, we can certainly prevent people from exploiting children, since we don't recognize them as fully autonomous.

PETER: Kant does say that we must respect humanity in *ourselves* as well as others. We have a duty to respect ourselves as well. So I suspect that the duty of self-respect could be used as the basis for morally condemning participation in pornography, if we take such participation to be a kind of servile acceptance of being used as a mere thing to promote others' pleasure.

ANTHONY: But what about privacy? What if I want to read pornographic literature in the privacy of my home? Shouldn't that be my moral right? I wouldn't be exploiting anyone. Or how about the use of a recreational drug like marijuana? That doesn't hurt anyone.

PETER: We have talked about this before. In both of these cases, I suppose it depends on whether your act would have damaging social consequences or whether by doing these things you would directly or indirectly fail to respect other persons. In any case, I think you're right to see that *if* you take autonomy to be your fundamental ethical value, then the right to be "left alone," the right to privacy, would be at the center of your moral viewpoint.

MARK: There are numerous court cases in which the right to privacy or personal rights have to be weighed against other considerations.

PETER: Often, utilitarian considerations. The nonconsequentialist is suspicious of our ability to judge what is *the* good for people and to calculate accurately the consequences of action, so he takes as most fundamental the right to his own considered judgment, the right not to be coerced, even by well-intentioned people who want to maximize goodness.

SOPHIA: But this can be taken to an extreme. Sometimes people choose things for themselves that don't harm others, but they do harm themselves. Do we simply stand by and let people become drug addicts, or destroy their lives by gambling, or get their brains smashed in motorcycle accidents because they don't have sense enough to wear a helmet?

SARAH: Or how about boxing? I love sports but I can't stand to watch boxers try to beat each other senseless. I know they can make money, but all the medical evidence shows that boxing can cause severe brain damage. Look at poor Muhammad Ali. I feel so sorry for him.

BOB: I suspect the issue of euthanasia, or at least some types of decisions about death, would turn on the issue of autonomy. If you stressed autonomy and a person wanted to end his life because of a very painful terminal illness, wouldn't we have to accept his decision? That's a position I still cannot accept and my church cannot accept.

SOPHIA: I have no problems with that. In some cases, I think it's cruel not to accept the wishes of the dying.

PETER: Look at our discussion. I can't stress too much that even when we seem to have discovered a profoundly important ethical principle that illuminates our moral life, numerous difficulties remain. We have to understand how the principle applies to the difficult situations of real life, and for that we need judgment. Even more important, just as we saw when we discussed consequentialism, we face the troubling question of whether all aspects of our moral life are illuminated by this perspective. Surely consequentialist moral reasoning isn't irrelevant. We started that discussion by talking about how plausible it is, how common it is, to think about how our actions affect the sum total of others' lives. Now we are talking about respecting persons, but we seem not to be able to bury the relevance of utilitarian considerations.

SOPHIA: Then why not have both? Does one theory have to be *the* correct moral theory?

PETER: Certainly, proponents of the theories sometimes claim them to be. Notice that as soon as you say that there are *two* fundamental perspectives in morality you face all the problems of weighing the two in your concrete moral decisions.

BOB: But in utilitarianism you also have to balance competing goods or different moral rules.

PETER: Yes. As I have said, moral theories may synthesize, they may illuminate, they may be practically useful, but they do not abolish completely the burdens and the difficulties of moral choice.

SOPHIA: I have one remaining question. It occurred to me when Mark was talking a few moments ago. He seemed to be very sympathetic to the respect for persons principle, since it seemed to carve out a space for individuals to do their own thing. We know that he is sympathetic to egoism. Now I can imagine him accepting the fact that you can't use other people, you can't exploit them, but above all you have to respect their freedom, their liberty. If people live their own lives and don't explicitly violate the rights of others, then that would be acceptable. What about charity? Helping others? It leads to a kind of moral minimalism, doesn't it? You can't harm others, but you don't necessarily have to help them, either. Do you see what I'm getting at?

PETER: Yes, I do.

SOPHIA: And it's reflected here in our own society. We talk more about protecting individual rights than our duty to be caring and sensitive to others, to help them, not to turn our backs on the suffering right here at home.

PETER: In philosophical language, you think Kant's perspective might overly emphasize the duty to leave people alone or the duty not to overtly harm them, at the expense of the duty to promote goodness, or the duty to directly help their lives.

SOPHIA: That's it. For Kant, shouldn't we help others?

PETER: Remember that this perspective demands that we treat people fairly when good is distributed, so the duty to be just will obviously directly affect people's lives. But your point is well taken. One of Kant's famous examples concerns our duty to help others in distress. Clearly, if it *is* a duty, he thinks it follows from his respect for persons principle as well as his universalizability principle. He holds that treating humanity as an end in itself requires that I embrace the ends of others, that I make the ends of others *my* ends.

MARK: I don't see that. That's not the way I understand the term "respect." I can respect you without liking you, or helping you. It's as if Kant is saying that respecting people means that I must make the purposes of all other persons my own purposes. That sounds more like utilitarianism, where everyone's good is equal to my own and I have to try to produce the most good for everybody concerned.

SARAH: I see what Mark is getting at. I had a coach in college whom I *respected*, but I didn't like her at all. It's not like she was my friend. It was hard to feel positive about her, but she was a good coach.

SOPHIA: That's an excellent way of thinking about this. What are we supposed to *feel* toward others if we respect them? If we don't actively help others, are we denying the respect they deserve, or is it something different?

PETER: Let me give you an example. There are millions of hungry people in the world, huge numbers of people, including children, who die of malnutrition and starvation. I would wager that few of you give as much as you can to organizations that attempt to help these people. I'd wager that most of you buy luxuries quite often and give no thought to the fact that you could use that money to combat world hunger. My question is this: By failing to give money to fight world hunger, do you fail to "respect" these people, or are you *using* them in some way? On the other hand, if you aren't using them, do you feel you are doing all that is morally required of you in relation to the starving of the world?

MARK: I don't think I'm using anyone by failing to give to charity. That's what it is—charity.

PETER: As opposed to . . . ?

BOB: As opposed to duty?

PETER: So it's beyond duty, Mark?

MARK: Yes. I admit that it's nice when people give, but it's their money. It's up to them. They have a right to do what they want with their money.

SOPHIA: I see what the example is getting at. I think I agree that not giving isn't a failure to respect starving people, but I think we ought to give. They *are* people, and we should feel something for them. They live in miserable, wretched conditions, while we wear our Gucci loafers and drive our expensive cars.

PETER: What would the consequentialist say? Should we give to charity?

ALICE: Of course. If it doesn't hurt us and it would help others, we should give.

ANTHONY: What do you think, Peter?

PETER: I'm unsure about whether respect entails that we have obligations to aid the needy or to give to charity, but I believe we do have such obligations. So I'm not inclined to think that the principle of respect covers all of our obligations. It seems to me that, whether Kant himself held this or not, respect is a kind of attitude we take toward others. I'm struck by your examples. Recall that Mill wanted to associate utilitarianism with the Christian ethic of love. It does seem that if my attitude toward others is one of love, rather than respect, much more is required of me in terms of actively contributing to the lives of other beings.

SOPHIA: I think of the Buddhist emphasis on compassion toward all living things. It seems to me that compassion is very different from respect. If I have compassion for you, I really feel something toward you. It's almost like sympathy.

PETER: That's a fascinating remark. It suggests to me another line of criticism that is worth considering. You say that the Buddha promoted compassion toward *all* living things. Compare this with the injunction to love your neighbor. There is controversy whether this principle, which even appears in the Old Testament, is really universal. Nietzsche says, for example, the challenge should be to love the "farthest." St. Francis notwithstanding, the Buddhist extension of compassion to nonpersons is striking. Think about this in relation to Kant's emphasis on respect for *persons*. What is it that we're supposed to respect?

MARK: The liberty of people. The fact that they can choose.

PETER: Again, on what basis?

BOB: Reasons. Moral reasons.

PETER: Kant asks us to respect the rationality of persons. Evidently, for Kant, only rational agents are to be objects of moral consideration. He felt that we have no direct duties to animals. According to Kant, mistreating animals might cause us to mistreat humans, but there is nothing intrinsically wrong about being cruel to animals. This seems to me to be radically mistaken, and it appears to follow from the emphasis on rationality as the basis for moral consideration. I realize you'll probably all find this very controversial, but I quite agree with Bentham, the father of utilitarianism, who held that sentiency, the capacity to feel pain, is the basis for considering a being morally, considering its interests. As he said, when we consider the moral status of animals, we shouldn't ask, "Can they reason?" or "Can they talk?" but "Can they suffer?" I do think we should respect persons as rational, self-determining beings, but I also think we should be sensitive to the way our actions, or nonactions, affect the lives of beings whose status as "persons" is questionable.

BOB: Including fetuses? And the severely retarded?

PETER: Yes. Making rationality the center of your moral viewpoint appears to be somewhat incomplete.

SOPHIA: So are we back to consequentialism?

PETER: Only in the sense that we have deepened our understanding of its incompleteness as well as its relevance. Thanks for an enjoyable evening. I'm growing weary.

SARAH: You're weary? I'm exhausted, and my feet are tired.

PETER: My mind is tired. Good evening, everyone.

What Thinkers Have Said

But what sort of law can that be, the conception of which must determine the will, even without paying any regard to the effect expected from it, in order that this will may be called good absolutely and without qualifications? As I have deprived the will of every impulse which could arise to it from obedience to any law, there remains nothing but the universal conformity of its actions to law in general, which alone is to serve the will as a principle, i.e. I am never to act otherwise than so that I could also will that my maxim should become a universal law. Here, now, it is the simple conformity to law in general, without assuming any particular law applicable to certain actions, that serves the will as its principle, and must so serve it, if duty is not to be a vain delusion and a chimerical notion. The common reason of men in its practical judgments perfectly coincides with this and always has in view the principle here suggested.

Immanuel Kant, *Fundamental Principles of the Metaphysics of Morals*

If then there is a supreme practical principle or, in respect of the human will, a categorical imperative, it must be one which, being drawn from the conception of that which is necessarily an end for everyone because it is an end in itself, constitutes an objective principle of will, and can therefore serve as a universal practical law. The foundation of this principle is: rational nature exists as an end in itself. Man necessarily conceives his own existence as being so: so far then this is a subjective principle of human actions. But every other rational being regards its existence similarly, just on the same rational principle that holds for me: so that it is at the same time an objective principle, from which as a supreme practical law all laws of the will must be capable of being deduced. Accordingly the practical imperative will be as follows: So act as to treat humanity, whether in thine own person or in that of any other, in every case as an end withal, never as means only. . . .

Immanuel Kant, *Fundamental Principles of the Metaphysics of Morals*

"*Respect for persons*" is therefore a principle which summarizes the attitude which we must adopt towards others with whom we are prepared seriously to discuss what ought to be done. Their point of view must be taken into account as sources of claims and interests; they must be regarded as having a prima facie claim for noninterference in doing what is in their interest; and no arbitrariness must be shown towards them as participants in discussion. To have the concept of a person is to see an individual as an object of respect in a form of life which is conducted on the basis of those principles which are presuppositions of the use of practical reason. . . .

R. S. Peters, "Respect for Persons and Fraternity"

Let us now try to tie together the various components in our attitude of respect. Insofar as persons are thought of as self-determining agents who pursue objects of interest to themselves, we respect them by showing active sympathy with them; in Kant's language, we make their ends our own. Insofar as persons are thought of as rule-following, we respect them by taking seriously the fact that the rules by which they guide their conduct constitute reasons which may apply both to them and to ourselves. In the attitude of respect we have, then, two necessary components: an attitude of active sympathy and a readiness at least to consider the applicability of other men's rules both to them and to ourselves. These two components are independently necessary and jointly sufficient to constitute the attitude of respect which it is fitting to direct at persons, conceived as rational wills.

R. S. Downie and Elizabeth Telfer, *Respect for Persons*

Key Terms and Concepts

what if everyone did that?

absolute rules

universalizability

arbitrariness

conflict of duties

respect for persons

treating merely as means

persons vs. things

unconditional worth vs. conditional worth

dignity

autonomy

moral minimalism

Questions

1. How "absolute" are moral rules? What does "absolute" mean?

2. What moral criticism is involved when one responds to an action by asking, "What if everyone did that?"

3. Explain why some moral rules are self-defeating when they are universalized. Give an example.

4. Give examples of a conflict between two supposedly "absolute" moral rules. How is such a conflict resolved?

5. Would you say that conventional or commonsense morality is more closely associated with consequentialism or Kantianism?

6. Use some examples to formulate a clearer conception of "treating someone merely as a means." That is, try to elaborate more fully what this principle means.

7. Explain the difference between persons and things.

8. Is it ever morally permissible to interfere with a person's autonomy?

9. Do you believe that "respecting" persons entails that you must positively help them, not merely refrain from hurting them?

10. Are there other kinds of beings, besides persons, that we ought to "respect"? Why or why not? If there are, what kind of "respect" is due?

Suggested Readings

Donagan, Alan, *The Theory of Morality*, University of Chicago Press, 1977. An important defense of deontology.

Downie, R. S., and Telfer, Elizabeth, *Respect for Persons*, Schocken Books, 1970. The source of the final quotation.

Feldman, Fred, *Introductory Ethics*, Prentice-Hall, 1978. His treatment of Kant is especially good. Our discussion of "What if everyone did that?" is indebted to the way he introduces students to the categorical imperative.

Frankena, William, *Ethics*, 2nd ed. Prentice-Hall, 1973. Contains a readable defense of a "mixed deontological" theory, combining a principle of beneficence and a principle of justice.

Kant, Immanuel, *Foundations of the Metaphysics of Morals*, trans. by Lewis White Beck, Bobbs-Merrill, 1959. The enormously influential defense of deontology.

Peters, R. S., *Ethics and Education*, Scott, Foresman and Company, 1967. The source of the third quotation.

Ross, W. D., *The Right and the Good*, Oxford University Press, 1930. Sympathetic critic of Kant whose theory of *prima facie* duties was an important contribution to deontological ethics.

Dialogue Seven:
Ethics and Virtue

The party finally arrives at Lost Lake, the destination of their hike, where they will relax for a few days. They meet two Jesuit priests, who are professional philosophers and who are acquaintances of Sophia. The two Jesuits defend the position that virtue is primary in our moral lives. Virtue depends on the notion that living well involves developing good habits of choosing what is really good for us. The discussion involves an important analysis of human happiness according to the teleological tradition associated with Aristotle and Aquinas. The dialogue ends with reflections about the place of God in such an approach and about the modern notion of the moral point of view.

SARAH: I promised you a beautiful view.

BOB: You said it.

RANSOM: Let's drink it in for a while. If we go a little farther around the lake, the view will become even more spectacular, and we can find a place to make camp. We'll walk past those fellows fishing.

MARK: Fellows fishing?

ALICE: I thought we'd be up here by ourselves.

SARAH: Well, there's a rugged back trail that four-wheel vehicles can take. Sometimes fishermen from the town come up that way. It's not an everyday thing, though. It's still a commitment and a heck of a journey that way, too.

As the party hikes around the lake, the two fishermen take note and walk toward them. In time, the anglers, dressed in peculiar plaids, hail Sarah's group. The hikers march toward them.

SOPHIA: Oh my gosh. I thought I recognized those voices. It's Jack and Steve.

JACK: I told you, Sophia, that we might meet you here. But we were about to give up on you. Steve here has just about "fished-out" this lake.

SARAH: You haven't been using explosives, have you?

JACK: [Laughing.] Believe me, the fish would have a better chance if Steve used hand grenades. He ties the meanest fly in the Rockies.

RANSOM: Should we go collect pine cones, or are you going to introduce us to these gentlemen, Sophia?

SOPHIA: Sorry. Everybody, I'd like you to meet two friends of mine, Jack Martin and Steve Gilliam. They're a couple of Jesuits from back home. I worked with them last year through our community ecumenical council.

BOB: You guys came all this way just to welcome Sophia to Lost Lake?

JACK: Well, not exactly. You see, the Jesuits in our community vacation in this area every year. We have a villa behind those mountains.

SOPHIA: In fact, Jack and Steve were the first to tell me about this area. And when I read that the university was sponsoring an excursion here, I signed up. They told me last spring that they might be here during our trip. They knew that we'd be here, too, because they are both campus ministers at the university.

PETER: Of course, I recognize you gentlemen now. In fact, Jack used to teach in our department as an adjunct.

JACK: That was years ago, I'm afraid.

SOPHIA: Actually, both Jack and Steve have taught at several schools in the Midwest.

STEVE: [Laughing.] Yeah. Let's not go into why we've taught at several instead of one.

BOB: Wait a minute. You're telling me that we've stumbled across more philosophers?

ROSE: If you fellows had known what we've been up to these past ten days, you'd have run away when you saw us hiking up the trail. I'm afraid that you're going to get involved in some deep thinking if you stay around this group.

BOB: Yeah. I'm not sure that's what you had in mind, but there's no escape for you now.

SOPHIA: You see, fellows, by day Ransom and Sarah have been guiding us around the hazards of the mountains, but by night Peter has been guiding us around the pitfalls of moral philosophy.

STEVE: Really? That's great. You've found the right company. Jack here has been talking for days about a book he's writing. It's a book on ethics no less.

BOB: I'm really glad to meet you two. I'm sure you'll be able to shed further light on our conversations. I'm anxious to hear what you have to say. I'm sure with your Jesuit backgrounds that you're familiar with the philosophies of Aristotle and Aquinas. I'd like to hear how their philosophies apply to some of the views we've been discussing. I know a little about their thought, because, you see, I've spent a few summers . . .

SOPHIA: Let us tell them for you, Bob. Everybody now: Bob's spent a few summers at the Aspen Institute with Dr. Adler!

ROSE: Sophia!

BOB: Have I told you that before?

SOPHIA: Try for triple digits, Cosmo.

STEVE: I, for one, am impressed, Bob. If you're sympathetic with Dr. Adler's work, we'll probably see eye to eye on a number of issues.

BOB: After we pitch camp later, I hope you can join us.

STEVE: I'm afraid we'll have to wait till tomorrow to get together. I'm tired. Those trout got the better of me today.

JACK: It's a dirty job catching all those fish, but somebody's got to do it. As for me, I'm tired from skipping stones, so I second the idea for meeting tomorrow.

SOPHIA: All right, but put all your skills on alert. Peter is in the big leagues, you know.

The following evening, Jack and Steve rejoin the campers.

SOPHIA: [Laughing.] How good of you guys to show up now that all the work is done.

BOB: We've been looking forward to your arrival. I've been trying to get the discussion off the ground, but they said they wouldn't budge until you got here.

PETER: I've been hoping that, once you gentlemen arrived, you could help us chart a new direction for conversation. I'd like to start by asking Jack to tell us about this ethics book he's writing. What inspired you to tackle such a project?

JACK: Frustration, I'm afraid. The idea for the book came as a response to my own difficulties at finding certain kinds of textbooks on ethics. As you know, textbook options can sometimes be really limited. That's especially true when you want to discuss ethics from the standpoint of virtue. Some of my colleagues expressed similar frustrations. So I was encouraged to write an ethics textbook on virtue; you know, to fill the void.

ROSE: Virtue. On no, don't tell me there's something else about ethics to talk about.

MARK: Yeah, there's no end to it.

SARAH: Wasn't that a line from *Deliverance?*

SOPHIA: This word "virtue" sounds pretty old-fashioned to me. It brings to mind images of Carrie Nation and the Temperance League.

JACK: Unfortunately, the term "virtue" is sometimes associated with priggish and puritanical morals, but that's no way to understand or to appreciate virtue ethics. In fact, the virtue of virtue, so to speak, is that it enables people to be very flexible about their moral decisions.

ALICE: You mean like situation ethics?

JACK: Well, I might not want to go that far. But virtue does put us in a position to make better moral sense of our situations, because it defines and forms our moral character. With this awareness of who and what we are morally, we can be more intelligent and can respond better to moral situations. In this way, virtue might be the key to minimizing the risk of error in moral choices.

SOPHIA: What do you mean by saying that virtue "defines our moral character"?

JACK: Think of the emphasis on virtue in our moral lives as a way of expressing that ethics is not only about doing but also about being. Or should I say that doing is largely determined by being?

SOPHIA: I can tell right now that we're going to be passing the baton to Peter, and soon.

STEVE: You'll have to forgive Jack. He prefers to talk in abstractions. He's the relentless metaphysician. If you're not careful, he'll get you to discuss how many angels dance on the head of a pin.

JACK: I apologize. Steve demonstrates his friendship by hitting me with those pig bladders now and then, keeping me down-to-earth. I'll do my best to keep my remarks simple and clear. Returning to the subject, I should also point out that a person's moral character, while it influences his choices and actions, is itself formed by those choices and actions. Virtues, then, are *habits* formed by making satisfactory moral decisions and acting on them. For example, you become honest and fair by behaving honestly and fairly. In time, such actions become second nature, enabling you to make satisfactory choices in the future, regardless of the circumstances you find yourself in. Anyway, that's how virtues are formed.

SOPHIA: And vices? I notice, Steve, that you're not smoking those strong cigars.

STEVE: No. Jack and I struck a deal out here for a few days. I don't smoke, and Jack eats the fish that I catch. Sounds like a fair trade, huh?

JACK: Steve conveniently forgot to tell you who cleans most of those fish. But seriously, Sophia, vices are the opposite of virtues.

Vices are habits for choosing and acting wrongly; you know, when you've cultivated a tendency to make bad decisions, when you've done bad things, like being cowardly, dishonest, or unjust.

ROSE: But how do you know when you've made a wrong choice?

PETER: Yes. That's the central question. That's what we've been trying to answer in our evening discussions. I'm delighted that we've met Jack and Steve, because I suspect that they're going to give us an answer to that question that we haven't heard before.

STEVE: To answer your question, Rose: Very generally, a person chooses and acts rightly when she or he chooses and acts according to right desire.

BOB: Yes. I remember this reference to right desire in Aristotle's *Nicomachean Ethics*, which we discussed at the institute.

PETER: But that isn't really very informative, is it? Shouldn't you tell us the meaning of "right desire"? If I recall, Aristotle never tells us what it means.

JACK: You're right about Aristotle. But the meaning of "right desire" appears in his text implicitly. A right desire is a desire you ought to have. What I would call a "real good."

PETER: So let me get this straight. A real good is what you ought to desire?

JACK: Correct.

PETER: But a right desire is also desiring what you ought to desire.

JACK: Right.

PETER: But that amounts to saying that a right desire consists in desiring what is really good. Aren't you just saying that what one ought to desire one ought to desire? But this is circular, Jack, which is to say nothing at all. What you have said thus far does not answer Rose's question.

JACK: Sophia, you're right. I'm playing in the big leagues now.

SOPHIA: Just roll up your sleeves, Jack. You're up to it.

STEVE: Don't worry, Jack. We'll play by World Wrestling Federation rules. Just tag me, and I'll jump in and tackle the Hulkster for you. For, you see, I think I have a response to Peter's keen objection that your argument is circular. The way out of this circle is to talk about what is really good in a way that does not simply repeat that it is what we ought to desire. This can be done by appealing to a basic distinction within the realm of desire. We should distinguish between *needs* and *wants,* or between *natural* and *acquired* desires.

JACK: Yes. Excellent clarification, Steve. To speak of objects of needs or natural desires, I use the expression "real goods." To refer to objects of wants or acquired desires, I use the expression "apparent goods."

STEVE: Just to make sure everyone understands what we're talking about, let me explain them this way: Real goods refer to desires so fundamental that without their fulfillment it is impossible for a person to live well as a human being. Nutrition, health, and knowledge are obvious examples. Without these, a person cannot lead a fully human life, a life that's happy. A real good, then, cannot help but be good for me. Apparent goods, however, are objects of desires that are more or less relative to individual taste and temperament, and, in fact, that may not really be good for me at all. That is to say, they may interfere with getting real goods. For example, if I choose to satisfy my nutritional need (a real good) by drinking two fifths of Jack Daniels every day (an apparent good), I'm obviously not acting sensibly. Why?

MARK: Because you're drinking Green Label instead of Black Label?

STEVE: Perhaps. But I think it's because my apparent good (what I want) clearly is not in this case a real good (what I need).

BOB: Well said, Steve. I remember Dr. Adler making a lot of this distinction. I think you've just given us the answer to Rose's question. Since a person can never go wrong in desiring what he needs, since he can never have too much of what he needs, the aims of right choices and right actions are real goods.

STEVE: Impressive, Bob. Folks, I think we're looking at a future recipient of the Aquinas medal. Ethics is about making sound, selective choices regarding apparent goods, so that they turn out to be real goods. And a person must cultivate virtues, good habits, such as prudence, courage, temperance, and justice, in order to make these satisfactory choices. As I have said, in life you have to determine whether what you want is really good for you or not. Virtue insures that you figure that out, and that you choose and act on those wants that accord with real goods and that you avoid choosing what interferes with the attainment of real goods. After all, the sum total of real goods is human happiness.

PETER: But isn't this talk about needs rather vague? I have needs and you have needs. But do we have identical needs?

SOPHIA: Yeah. Talk about needs on a general level is all very good. But when it comes to talk about particular needs, who are you to tell me what my needs are?

JACK: If the distinction between natural and acquired desires is valid, then any one of us can point to our common natural desires to identify the needs for a human life well lived, that is, a happy life. I'm not saying that there is not a place for individuality. But the subjectivity and relativity of human differences come into play with regard to our wants, not our needs. We all have the same needs, because our needs are rooted in human nature, which we all share. See, this is the beauty of my view. It puts ethics on an objective basis. Real goods are standards for a human life well lived. In this way, ethics overcomes relativism and subjectivism. There is one moral plan for every human life, whether ancient Greek or modern American: namely, to satisfy one's needs; that is, to obtain real goods.

PETER: I have a number of difficulties, gentlemen. So many, in fact, that I'm not sure where to begin. Let's start with your appeal to human nature. This leads to some genuine difficulties. In the first place, I am suspicious of any effort to establish this mysterious and metaphysical thing called "human nature." As you know, the idea of human nature has been out of fashion for some time in philosophy. I'm not in the habit of quoting continental philosophers, but the words of Merleau-Ponty come to mind: "It is the nature of man not to have a nature." I'm afraid that you're going to have to say more than you've said so far to convince us that there is a human nature. Second, even if we grant that human beings have a common nature, this really does nothing to help your ethical position. A correct claim about human nature is only a descriptive truth, and a descriptive truth is never adequate to justify a prescriptive claim, which is, of course, what an ethical theory attempts to do. Since you cannot derive the prescriptive from the descriptive, ought from is, your theory of human nature, even if true, does you no good.

STEVE: I'm not at all surprised to hear you question Jack's view of human nature. You're quite right to observe that the idea of human nature is out of step with modern philosophy. But there are still some oddballs such as Jack and I who escape the current trends and argue for human nature nonetheless.

PETER: Well, I'm willing to listen if you want to try to convince me.

JACK: If Steve will help, we can unpack this piece by piece. For starters, I understand why you might question whether there is a human nature. Your motive is no doubt based on a sensitivity to the history of philosophy. What I mean is this: It has unfortunately been the case that some philosophers in the past have treated human nature too abstractly, thinking of it as a kind of Platonic essence. In fact, I must confess that some of these culprits have belonged to my own tradition, a tradition I might label natural law ethics, for want of another expression. Too often, these thinkers have unwittingly regarded human nature as a kind of unchangeable form. And this serves their purpose beautifully when they want to put together a catalogue of inflexible moral prohibitions. You're quite right to reject this caricature of human nature. I think your reaction is healthy.

MARK: Whew. There's some deep shoveling that's going to happen here. I hope we can get a written transcript of this conversation.

STEVE: Fortunately, the caricature is not the only option. Some philosophers, like Aristotle and Aquinas, remind us that human nature really exists but not as a Platonic form. According to their view, human nature is only realized in distinct individuals, which is why ethics must, on some level, take into account individual differences, even if we do have the same nature. But there is human nature nonetheless. Regrettably, modern philosophers have paid far too much attention to the Platonic caricature rather than to the more sensible Aristotelian version. It has led them to reject human nature out of hand.

JACK: I would insist that the biologists are wiser than the contemporary philosophers and the social scientists who are on the whole doubtful about there being a human nature.

SOPHIA: What do you mean, Jack? Why the biologists?

JACK: The biologists, you see, are still quite willing to separate humankind from the other animals on grounds that we possess certain genetic characteristics that differentiate us as a species. We are the species *homo sapiens*.

BOB: How about the social scientists?

STEVE: He's talking about the psychologists, sociologists, political scientists, and anthropologists. They generally suspect, and often reject, the notion of human nature.

ALICE: What is there about social scientists that makes them suspicious about a philosophy of human nature?

STEVE: One reason has to do with what Jack said earlier. Like many philosophers, social scientists have rejected moral philosophies based on an abstract and fixed notion of human nature. But another reason is that social science has its own unique history. Early anthropological researchers were struck by the diversity of cultural beliefs and practices, and this seemed to compel them to ignore common factors in human experience, factors that seem to indicate that there is a human nature.

SOPHIA: You two missed our discussion on relativism.

BOB: We talked about the problems for the relativist when he exaggerates the differences among cultures.

JACK: Then you appreciate Steve's point. Anyway, for a number of historical reasons, belief in human nature is not fashionable today, at least not among the philosophers and social scientists. But I believe that such intellectuals are mistaken. I think one can make a convincing case that there is such a thing as human nature, and one can do so without appealing to the "mysterious" or the "metaphysical."

SOPHIA: Excuse me for interrupting, but surely human nature involves the metaphysical, because aren't *you* committed at least to the view that God creates this nature?

PETER: Yes. Isn't that one of the reasons some philosophers have been attracted to the idea of human nature, that it involves God?

JACK: But it doesn't need to involve God. I'm not talking about the origin of human nature; I'm just simply making a case that there is human nature. Whether it comes about by evolution or by God's creative act . . .

BOB: Or both!

JACK: . . . is not the issue here. Anyway, the origin of human nature is not what I'm trying to address—only that there is human nature. And my argument for human nature is that there are capacities or potentialities shared by all human beings. Since these capacities are also human desires, since without their fulfillment human beings are prevented from living as well as they can, they relate, naturally, to real goods. Real goods are the objects of right desire and they are the key to human happiness. Now there is nothing mystical about these potentialities. They are evident in any human life, and any conscious person is at least implicitly aware of them.

PETER: And what, pray tell, are these common potentialities?

JACK: They are capacities of body and mind shared by all human beings. Some of them, we've mentioned already. For example, human beings have certain nutritional capacities; if these are not satisfied, human beings live deficient lives, or, at worst, they may die. Quite simply, human beings need food and water. There are other bodily capacities or needs. For example, we need health, vigor, and even some physical pleasure in life. In addition, there are common capacities of the mind that must be fulfilled, if a person is to be happy, such as love and knowledge. Also, a person has certain capacities that can only be realized in an appropriate social and political environment. For example, a person needs a certain amount of freedom in order to live well. Human needs, then, provide a standard enabling us to judge between good and bad societies.

STEVE: Jack has said two things here. First, he has said we have these common capacities that establish human nature. Second, he has said that these capacities are also natural desires or needs. They ought to be satisfied, then, if we are to live lives that we would call genuinely and fully human.

JACK: And virtues are necessary for making the choices that enable us to satisfy these natural desires for ourselves and others.

PETER: I'm not so sure that just identifying common potentialities justifies that we have a human nature.

STEVE: I suspect that you're still worried that human nature has to be some kind of Platonic form. But human nature is just the presence of traits common to all human beings. These characteristics, I argue, happen to be common potentialities. If we actualize them, we live well as a human being.

JACK: It is worth noting that not all of these potentialities that comprise human nature are unique to human beings. Some of them, such as capacities for growth, nutrition, and sense knowledge, other creatures also share. But some of our characteristics are unique, such as capacities for intellectual knowledge and free choice.

STEVE: I am hopeful, Peter, that these remarks show that human nature is not the invention of some metaphysical theory, such as

Platonism; instead it is the awareness that human beings share certain traits, some of which they uniquely share.

PETER: Well, it makes no difference whether or not one accepts that there is a human nature. As I said earlier, human nature cannot support a moral theory, since a descriptive truth cannot justify a prescriptive conclusion.

JACK: To that objection, Peter, let me say this: I challenge the assumption that there is such a thing as a descriptive truth in the first place. Truth is a value. A truth claim is a normative judgment. Truth is also another word for knowledge. And knowledge is a real good, an object of right desire. As a result, the is-ought controversy is a pseudoproblem. What I deny is the assumption that my moral philosophy is proposing that there is a transition from "is" to "ought." You see, it seems to me that in moral experience we are already in the realm of "ought"; we're not first waiting offstage, hoping someday to be called to perform; we are already on the moral stage, if you will. Simply by virtue of being human, with natural desires, we are already enveloped in the realm of value. My human potentialities are desires, including the desire for knowledge. And this brings me to a very important point: Since a desire may or may not be fulfilled, I must distinguish between real and apparent goods. This is the challenge of moral life, making decisions so that my apparent goods are real goods. To make those decisions, I need virtue, a highly developed ability for choosing what is really good for me.

STEVE: I would like to add a few comments of my own to what Jack has said. First, I'm not sure I would want to go as far as Jack in denying that there are descriptive truths. Let's grant your point on that for the sake of argument, Peter. You may be quite right in echoing David Hume that one cannot derive a prescriptive judgment from a descriptive one. But one certainly can derive a prescriptive judgment from a prescriptive one. And just as in any science, since you can't prove everything (that is, you have to start with something), so in ethics there must be a first principle. That starting point is a self-evident prescriptive truth, a prescriptive truth that serves as the basis of all other prescriptive claims. Mortimer Adler, as Bob probably knows, has argued this point, and convincingly, I think. Adler asks us to keep in mind the distinction between natural and acquired desires. In light of this distinction, he maintains that there is a self-evident prescriptive judgment: namely, that one ought to desire whatever is really good, and nothing else.

PETER: And why is that proposition self-evident?

STEVE: The reason is that one cannot think its opposite. Can you imagine, Peter, a person thinking he should desire what is really bad for him? Or that he ought not to desire what is really good for him? The very meaning of "really good" implies that one should desire it. Since this has to do with the actual meaning of the terms, it is impossible to think of "really good" and "ought" being related in any other way.

PETER: But where does your philosophy of human nature figure into this?

JACK: I think I can respond to that question. It's a matter of understanding descriptive claims about human nature in the light of the self-evident prescriptive truth Steve has mentioned. If it's a self-evident prescriptive truth that one ought to desire whatever is really good for a person, we can combine with this proposition descriptive truths (granting that the notion of descriptive truth makes sense in the first place) and thereby justify moral conclusions. For example, we can combine with our self-evident prescriptive truth the descriptive truth that all human beings naturally desire to know (just to mention one human potentiality among others), and thereby we can derive the conclusion that a person ought to seek or desire knowledge.

STEVE: Our position is not vulnerable to Hume's criticism that one cannot derive "ought" from "is." In my judgment, Hume has not properly understood the prescriptive foundations of morality, and therefore has passed to posterity another pointless controversy.

PETER: As you may suspect, I have further reservations, but Sophia is wanting to say something.

SOPHIA: I've been wanting to ask about one particular word that Jack and Steve have used. That word is "happiness." And you say we've got to have virtues to get it. Just what do you mean by happiness? I heard Steve earlier connect happiness with real goods, but I'm not sure I can accept that. Real goods are what everybody, so you say, needs; but don't we think of happiness as what we want? Isn't happiness a very individual thing? I mean, doesn't it vary from person to person? Surely, you're not suggesting that what makes me happy makes you or another person happy.

STEVE: I'm not suggesting it; I'm declaring it. Remember, individuality in our moral life figures in when we make choices regarding what we want. But happiness is clearly more than just getting what we want. What we want has to be really good for us, otherwise our human nature is not perfected and we are not, then, happy. If happiness were just a matter of getting what we want, then we could call a miser happy. He has what he wants. But morally he is a stunted and pathetic creature. Quite reasonably, we do not call him happy, because what he wants does not agree with what he *ought* to want.

PETER: Wait a minute, gentlemen. This leads to an odd confusion. If happiness is not getting what we want, then happiness becomes something that is not happy.

JACK: What do you mean?

PETER: Well, what happens when a person doesn't get what he wants?

SOPHIA: He becomes frustrated.

PETER: Frustration, then, becomes an ally of our happiness. But this is unacceptable, since we ordinarily speak of our frustrations as impediments to our happiness. That is to say, ordinarily we speak of becoming frustrated when our happiness, what we want, cannot be gotten.

JACK: I think I can reply to that. We should make a distinction, one that has been lost on the minds of modern philosophers, and on popular culture as well. Dr. Adler has argued that we should understand the difference between happiness as a *norm* and happiness as a *terminus*. Modern philosophers think of happiness as a terminus, as a psychological state of contentment that one can attain and rest in. According to this meaning of "happiness," the concept is equated with a life of enjoyment. Now, admittedly, if you accept that concept of happiness, you will have difficulty accepting my view that real goods define happiness, since my view may require a life in which what one wants should be sacrificed to what one needs (what one ought to want). This may require a life with episodes, perhaps even lengthy episodes, of unenjoyable experiences.

BOB: Oh, I think I get it. Happiness is not so much a matter of life lived from moment to moment, but rather a matter of life lived as a whole.

STEVE: Right again, Bob. What Jack is saying here goes to the very heart of the difference between an Aristotelian moral philosophy and modern theories. On the Aristotelian view, happiness is not one good among others; it is rather the sum total of all goods obtained. Happiness, then, is the end sought in our lives, but normatively, as a standard telling us whether our choices are sound or not. But it is not a particular good, a particular state, that one can obtain and rest in, at least not in this life.

SOPHIA: Ah ha! I had a suspicion that religion would sneak in at some point.

STEVE: Well, it is appropriate to the discussion in certain respects. But I'd prefer to touch on that later. The point I'm making now about happiness is summed up in Aristotle's bold remark that we can call no man happy until he is dead. What he means by this is that happiness is a norm that is operative in a person's entire life, not a state or condition that he attains. It's a norm that can be used retrospectively to evaluate whether a person's life, now looked upon as whole, was happy or not.

SOPHIA: I think I'm beginning to see what you're saying, but I'm still fuzzy on this "terminal" and "normative" stuff.

JACK: Perhaps an illustration might help. An example of a terminal goal would be a destination of a trip. Your trip to Lost Lake, for instance. You plan the trip, you initiate the journey, and you arrive at your destination. Once there, you may enjoy your arrival, take in the beautiful scenery, and delight in resting at your destination. An example of a normative end is quite different. Take the case of a ballet performance. The performance is a process, which is performed according to a standard of excellence. But one can only truly judge whether this end or norm is met when the performance is over. And yet that goal is as much a factor in the performance of the ballet as your desire to get to Lost Lake is a factor in your journey. But the latter kind of goal, a terminus, is something that can be attained and rested in; the former is not attainable in that way, since it is a standard or norm for a process, an activity, and it is a standard that only fully applies when the activity is over.

STEVE: Another example. If I asked you after the first half of the Rose Bowl whether this was an excellent game, I would not at all be puzzled if you answered me this way: "It has been played well so far, but I can't truly call it an excellent game until it's finished." The game cannot be fully assessed by the norm of excellence until it is completely played. So in life. Not until life is finished can it be wholly measured by the standard of happiness.

MARK: Help me out. What's the point?

JACK: The point of all this is that happiness should not be thought of as contentment, or as some other pleasant psychological state. It is a normative, not a psychological, principle. The latter refers to a state of satisfaction that can be attained, however impermanently, and rested in whenever one gets what he or she wants. But what Steve and I are arguing is that happiness should be thought of as the *totum bonum,* not as one good among many, that is, not as a good that can be achieved and rested in.

STEVE: As Jack pointed out, it may be the failure of modern thinkers to appreciate Aristotle's insight—that happiness is a normative principle rather than a terminal one—that has led modern moral theories down blind alleys, such as hedonism and utilitarianism, which mistake happiness for a psychological state, a state of contentment.

JACK: It has also led modern thinkers to misunderstand virtue. Virtue is not just a means to pleasure or contentment or some other terminal value; virtue is a condition for a whole life lived well. We need to be prudent, for example, in order to choose intelligently appropriate means for particular goals. When taken all together, these goals constitute our ultimate end, happiness. When such means involve taking risks, then the virtue of courage is necessary. When such means require moderation, then the habit of temperance is necessary. Of course, we are not born into this world alone. Human nature is also social and political. This means that how we relate to others is a factor in our own happiness. As a result, the virtue of justice is necessary to create a social order in which everybody's pursuit of real goods is valued.

STEVE: It should also be added that, if virtue is a condition for a whole life to be lived well, all the virtues must be perfected and present in an individual's life and conduct. It is not enough to have cultivated only a few of them. Such a person does not have an integrated moral character. This is a person who frustrates rather than fosters her happiness.

SOPHIA: But that can't be right. Don't we all have our faults? Can't we still be good people, even if we fall short and have a few vices?

JACK: Yeah. This is some idea coming from a guy who smokes ten cigars a day.

STEVE: Hey, I smoke those cigars just so I can use them as handy moral illustrations when circumstances such as this arise. Here they serve the purpose of showing that knowledge is not the same as virtue. I know better than to smoke them, but other factors, such as desire for pleasure and other passions, prevent me from acting on my knowledge. Moral knowledge only tells us what we ought to do (or ought not to do). And we ought to have developed all the virtues. If you have a few good habits, that's commendable, but that alone is not sufficient for you to be a good person, a person of integrity (meaning integrated moral habits, by the way), a person of fully developed moral character. Let me put it this way: A virtue aims at one's good, but a vice aims at evil (even though an apparent good), something that undermines one's good. Therefore, if one's life contains vice, then one is prone to make decisions that work against the good sought by virtuous acts. The combination of vice and virtue confuses the project of moral life and creates a kind of internal war in one's developing moral character. Thus, Aristotle rightly says that no man is virtuous until he has acquired all the virtues.

BOB: In terms of some specific virtues and vices, how does this conflict show up?

JACK: For example, the individual who eats too much or drinks excessively is foolish, because he is disposed to select a means for a wrong end. Likewise, the person who is unjust will not be prudent, however skillful he may be. He doesn't select appropriate means because his decisions are aimed at the wrong end, even if it *appears* to him to be the right end. Likewise, a person cannot be temperate and cowardly, or brave and intemperate. An individual cannot have a sensible moral life, if, on the one hand, he cultivates habits, such as courage and self-control, that dispose him toward his real good, and, on the other, he develops habits, such as carelessness and unfairness, that lead him away from what he ought to seek.

PETER: This language about means and ends leaves me uneasy. Virtues aim at our happiness. Happiness is an end, albeit a normative end, you say. It's an end, nonetheless. But this means that you're committed to a teleological ethics, the view that moral experience is judged by a standard that is an end, and that moral life, accordingly, is a means to an end. But if you subscribe to a teleological ethics, you have to defend it. Why is a teleological ethics justifiable in your view?

STEVE: We're getting into some heady waters here. But we can answer your question if you consider human action insofar as it is uniquely human. When human beings act in a human way, they act in a way that differentiates them from other creatures. They act according to capacities unique to them as human beings. It is true that humans and other creatures have many actions in common, for example, digesting, growing, seeing, hearing, and so forth. But we humans also have the capacity to act in ways peculiar to our nature, that is, according to powers unique to us, not shared by other creatures. Now it is clear that when a person acts in a uniquely human way, he has power over his actions. Freedom and intention show this. What this means is that we have dominion over our acts through reason and will. But will is the faculty of desire or appetite. Therefore, it requires the good as an object to move it. This means that when human beings act in a uniquely human way, they act for the good.

PETER: But why *the* good instead of just any good?

JACK: The reason is that, while we may desire many different goods, we desire each from the point of view that it is really good, that is, that it is really perfective or fulfilling of us. So when I say that we desire the good, I don't mean this in the sense of one particular good among others; I mean by "the good" what is common to any judgment about what is good: namely, that it is perfective or fulfilling of me, that is, a real good.

PETER: Doesn't this mean that happiness is that point of view under which any particular choice is made?

JACK: Well, the desire for happiness is that point of view. If we attain the totality of real goods, then we have achieved that desire. This is precisely what we mean when we say that happiness is a normative end.

PETER: I'm puzzled. You claim to be defending Aristotle's ethics, and yet your conception of happiness seems far broader than what I understand his to be. Doesn't he say that happiness is the perfection of our rational activity, so that the highest life attainable by human beings is the contemplative life? He says we even become godlike to the extent we perfect contemplation. This makes the life of the philosophy professor the highest and best kind of life.

RANSOM: Who would dispute that?

JACK: I don't want to bog down on a discussion of Aristotle's texts, but you've brought up an important point of interpretation. Aristotle is commonly misinterpreted, in my opinion, regarding his view of happiness. It is true that he says that rational activity is the life peculiar to the human person and is the life properly perfected for man. But his use of "rational activity" is what philosophers call "analogical." In other words, the expression "rational activity" covers a whole range of activities necessary for human beings to live genuinely human lives. The phrase "rational activity" not only refers to the operations of reason or intellect, but also refers to activities that come under the influence of reason. While the contemplative life may be the preeminent activity of the human person, it is not rightly the exclusive concern of any woman or man. It would actually be irrational to make it one's exclusive effort. At best, it can be achieved episodically. It would make no sense in a moral life to pursue it to the neglect of other human needs. In fact, one could never lead a contemplative life without heeding and taking care of his other needs. Interestingly, Aristotle himself makes this point by insisting that intellectual virtues presuppose the moral virtues. The human good is not one particular good—such as contemplation—among many; it is a plurality of real goods, like knowledge, friendship, health, and so forth, cumulatively attained. Aristotle has been much misunderstood on this point.

STEVE: Correct. What Aristotle is saying is that happiness is the *totum bonum*, not just one good. Happiness is a point of view, a standard according to which I can judge whether something is really fulfilling or perfective of me, that is, really good.

SOPHIA: But didn't you say that not everything we desire turns out to be really good?

JACK: Right. But that proves my point, doesn't it? Some things turn out to be only apparently good; they are not also really good. In other words, we can be mistaken. And when we discover that we are mistaken, we have a motive for changing our choices and actions. Not that we necessarily will. My knowledge of right desire alone is not sufficient to cause me to act rightly, my actions being too much governed, say, by passions and prejudice and perhaps other factors. This is, again, another way of saying that knowledge is not virtue. To know what you should do is not a sufficient condition for your actually doing it.

BOB: But I thought knowledge was virtue. Isn't knowledge a good habit, something a person ought to develop in life?

JACK: Yes. But knowledge is an intellectual or theoretical virtue, not a moral one.

BOB: What's the difference?

JACK: An intellectual virtue perfects our habit of thinking, whereas a moral virtue perfects our habit of acting. Wisdom and right reasoning are examples of theoretical virtues, but prudence and courage are instances of moral virtue.

SOPHIA: So that's all there is to it. Learn how to act like good boys and girls and, presto, you've got it all. Get moral virtue and you get happiness. I see every day what bunk that is. Good people get the shaft, while villains become the pillars of our community, and sleep like babies to boot! You guys have been talking among yourselves too long. Wake up and smell the coffee.

STEVE: I understand and appreciate your point. And it is a strong objection against some philosophies. But it does not apply to mine, for I am not saying that virtue is a sufficient condition for happiness, only that it is a necessary one. Your objection applies to the philosophies of Plato and the Stoics, who think that happiness is guaranteed if one acquires virtue.

JACK: Yes. These philosophers go to such extremes that they even believe a virtuous person could be content even while being tortured on the rack!

PETER: No doubt a very good person on a very bad rack.

STEVE: This Platonic view is very naive, for it runs contrary to our commonsense awareness that the attainment of happiness depends on more than just virtue. To be happy, one must also be lucky. Aristotle realized this and parted with Plato's moral philosophy on account of it.

JACK: As a result, Aristotle's position might be summed up this way: Happiness is the cumulative possession of all real goods attainable by virtue *and* good fortune in a complete life. Happiness is not a matter of virtue only.

SOPHIA: This point about the need for good fortune is important. It explains why programs like affirmative action are necessary.

STEVE: Exactly. We are in a sense at the mercy of the "natural lottery." A just society, that is to say, a society whose citizens are inspired by the virtue of fairness, will institute measures to try to help people who are disadvantaged, so that they, too, may have a life filled with the opportunity to develop those virtues that help make happiness attainable.

RANSOM: I've been sitting back listening to more of this attempt on the part of you philosophers to explain how we ought to live. You say that, if we do this, we'll perfect ourselves, but, if we do that, we'll ruin ourselves. The truth is that nobody's perfect except God, and that ultimately human well-being is a gift of God.

STEVE: You're quite right to point this out, Ransom. What Aristotle has given us is valid but also incomplete. The only happiness that human beings naturally (that is, on their own, without God) can attain is an imperfect happiness. Our perfection in this life is only a relative perfection.

SOPHIA: Ah ha. The other shoe drops. I suspected religion was behind all of this.

STEVE: I told you we'd get to it eventually, remember? But I should say that religion is not so much behind what I'm saying as it is in front of it. In other words, to be complete, a moral philosophy looks to religion to this extent: to take into account the *hope* of our supernatural union with God. For, you see, if the human will desires perfection, it can only be ultimately perfected by possessing God. God, then, is, strictly speaking, our true happiness, the *summum bonum*.

BOB: I see. You're saying that what we have said about happiness thus far, about it being the *totum bonum*, pertains only to our *natural* well-being.

PETER: You mean to say that God's existence is proven because our desire for perfection is not realizable in our natural lives? I find that very problematic.

STEVE: Not the existence of God, only the *need* of God. A person is free to believe in God or not, that human life can be supernaturally fulfilled by God or not. The point is that, because of the imperfections of our natural existence, faith has a certain rationale: Let us hope that our natural lives are related to a supernatural one so that our true happiness can be realized.

JACK: Maybe I can help clarify this by referring to one of Aquinas's arguments. It goes like this: No particular thing that we call good or no combination of particular goods is the Good or exhausts our desire for the Good. Hence, our desire, if it is to be satisfied, requires the attainment of the Good. The Good itself is not known in this life. Consequently, it is to be found, if at all, in another life.

STEVE: This argument that Jack has summarized is part of the rationale of Christian moral theology, which insists that, in addition to the philosophical virtues, such as prudence, courage, temperance, and justice, the moral life, if it is to be complete, must also prepare for union with God. Since this cannot be done under our power, God himself secures this preparation by gracing us with certain theological virtues—the so-called "infused" virtues—of faith, hope, and charity. But, of course, we must be receptive to this grace.

PETER: This reference to charity reminds me of a criticism I wanted to bring up earlier. It has to do with the moral point of view. It seems to me that your position doesn't adequately include the moral point of view. This strikes me as a deficiency in your account of philosophical morality. Perhaps this really prevents your account from being a morality at all, for morality is not mere prudentialism, that is, it is not pursuing merely one's own good.

SOPHIA: Touché. That's exactly what I've been thinking.

PETER: According to your view, the point of ethics is for the individual to attain his personal good. But where does this leave room for the moral point of view? Haven't you reduced the whole of moral philosophy to an egoism dressed up in a lot of fancy Aristotelian language?

JACK: To respond, let me say first that the virtue of justice is committed to the moral point of view. Justice requires a certain impartiality; it requires that we regard others as equal human beings, with the same nature and the same natural desires. It is difficult to secure justice without a commitment to human nature; otherwise, our relationships with others become arbitrary. Justice demands that we respect and acknowledge the needs of other persons simply because their lives, like our own, are human, rooted in the same needs and in pursuit of the same real goods. It is true that by being just I help myself. But my motive may also be disinterested, even altruistic, in the sense that I acknowledge and appreciate objectively the nature of any human life, which is a life uniquely developed according to certain capacities that are also values.

STEVE: I'm glad you've brought up this point, Peter. It highlights another contrast between natural law ethics and modern moral theories. For, you see, this emphasis on "the moral point of view" is a peculiarity of modern moral philosophers. They seem to make too much of it. If a person questions this modernist approach, then he can appreciate ethics more comprehensively, retaining the moral point of view by putting it in its proper context. That context is an explanation of the right in light of the good. Modern philosophers, however, have sometimes incorrectly inverted this order. They often overlook that the right is only discernible because of a prior understanding of what is good for human life. This mistake is very evident in the philosophy of Kant, whose categorical imperative—while a noble sentiment, since it's just a reformulation of the Golden Rule—is an empty maxim unless it furnishes a statement about what the good is for human life. To the extent that modern moral philosophies have lost sight of this point, which ancient and medieval moral philosophies understood so well, they have repeatedly gone down blind alleys.

JACK: Actually, Peter, the reason I brought up the virtue of charity is that I am sensitive to the moral point of view. At bottom, the moral point of view is supplied by the infused virtue of charity. Perhaps we can think of it this way: Human appetite desires the Good above all else. But nothing we experience in this life is the Good itself. Also we desire the Good even above our own happiness. By seeing God in others, we can love them even more than ourselves. Thus, when one recognizes that faith ultimately is required to complete philosophical morality, then one can also appreciate how the infused virtue of charity reinforces the moral point of view in human relationships.

STEVE: To speak frankly, Peter, I suspect that the notion of the moral point of view is a principle that moral philosophers have borrowed from Christianity, and afterward they have been searching for a way to give it a secular defense. The irony of modern experiments in moral philosophy is that, without Christianity and its emphasis on the moral point of view, modern moral theory would lack its basic principles, vocabulary, and cultural context. Sometimes I wonder whether the only reason modern moral philosophy has an audience at all is that that audience is still sufficiently enculturated by Christianity so as to understand the basic vocabulary of modern moral discourse. To put it more cynically, modern moral philosophies parasitically live off a slowly atrophying Christian culture, an atrophy that they themselves are partly responsible for. The parasite has damaged the health of the host, and it may, in time, kill it.

JACK: I wonder how long the appeal to the moral point of view can carry any authority once the context out of which such a notion acquired its force, namely, Christian culture, disappears. In fact, I suspect that almost all important principles in modern moral and political discourse rely on or exploit our Judeo-Christian culture and tradition. Where will we be when Christendom is no longer there to give these principles their context?

SOPHIA: Well, I wish our friend Donovan were here. I have a feeling he'd have an idea; he might even like the alternative.

PETER: I fear that my old friend Donovan understood your point well and even accepted it. For him, God is dead. Speaking for myself, I still want to believe that we can offer a secular defense of the moral point of view. I'm not one of those who believe that our only option is between Christianity and Nietzsche.

STEVE: Who? Donovan?

PETER: Fill your cups, fellows. The coffee is ready again. Meanwhile, I'll tell you a tale about my days in graduate school and people I've met.

What Thinkers Have Said

Why then should we not say that he is happy who is active in accordance with complete virtue and is sufficiently equipped with external goods, not for some chance period but throughout a complete life? . . . Certainly the future is obscure to us, while happiness, we claim, is an end and something in every way final. If so, we shall call happy those among living men in whom these conditions are, and are to be, fulfilled. . . .

Aristotle, *Nicomachean Ethics,* Book I, 10

What affirmation and negation are in thinking, pursuit and avoidance are in desire; so that since moral virtue is a state of character concerned with choice, and choice is deliberate desire, therefore both the reasoning must be true and the desire right, if the choice is to be good, and the latter must pursue just what the former asserts. Now this kind of intellect and of truth is practical; of the intellect which is contemplative, not practical nor productive, the good and the bad state are truth and falsity respectively (for this is the work of everything intellectual); while of the part which is practical and intellectual the good state is truth in agreement with right desire.

Aristotle, *Nicomachean Ethics,* Book VI, 2

I answer that it is possible by means of human works to acquire moral virtues, in so far as they produce good works that are directed to an end not surpassing the natural power of man: and when they are acquired thus they can be without charity, even as they were in many of the Gentiles. But in so far as they produce good works in proportion to a supernatural last end, thus they have the character of virtue, truly and perfectly; and cannot be acquired by human acts, but are infused by God. Such like moral virtues cannot be without charity.

St. Thomas Aquinas, *Summa Theologiae,* II, I, Q. 65, a. 2

All our natural desires or needs are right desires, so we ought to want what we need, for those are the things that are really good for us. The one self-evident principle of moral philosophy is that we ought to seek everything that is really good for us and nothing else. The principle is undeniable because the opposite is unthinkable.

Mortimer Adler, "Ethics: Fourth Century B.C.
and Twentieth Century A.D."

The pursuit of happiness is selfish to the extent that the good life it aims at directly is one's own good life, not the good life of anybody else. But when we realize that we cannot succeed in the pursuit of happiness without considering the happiness of others, our self-interest becomes enlightened. We cannot be entirely selfish and succeed.

That is why, according to Aristotle, the two aspects of moral virtue that we have so far considered are not enough. In addition to temperance and courage there is justice. Justice is concerned with the good of others, not only of our friends or those whom we love, but of everyone else. Justice is also concerned with the good of the all-enveloping society in which we live—the society we call the state.

Mortimer Adler, Aristotle for Everybody

If we were tempted to think that we act in a historical vacuum, our decision and choice uninfluenced by what we are as a result of our past actions, the deed a simple matter of rational appraisal and appetitive pursuit, we would quickly be disabused of our optimism. The problem of the moral life is far more one of moral change or conversion than it is of performing an isolated act as it ought to be done. The depressing side of this realization is that it is very complicated to act in conflict with our past moral history; the sunny side is that, if our moral history exhibits a conformity with right reason, it is almost as hard for us to do something foolish and wrong.

If habit, the settled disposition to act in one way rather than another, is a fact of the moral life, it is obviously of the greatest consequence to acquire habits of the appropriate kind, good habits, virtues.

Ralph McInerny, Ethica Thomistica

Key Terms and Concepts

virtue	living well
vice	natural law
moral character	human nature
right desire	is-ought problem
real goods vs. apparent goods	self-evident truths
natural desires vs. acquired desires	happiness as a norm

happiness as a terminus

knowledge and virtue

teleological ethics

intellectual virtues

moral virtues

theological virtues

Questions

1. What is virtue? What is suggested, nowadays, when we speak of a "virtuous" person? (Recall Sophia's comment early in the dialogue.)

2. What is the difference between real and apparent goods? Give as many examples as you can.

3. What is the relationship between virtue and goodness, according to Jack and Steve?

4. Explain how certain central virtues might lead us to the attainment of real goods.

5. Summarize the response to Peter's doubts about human nature and the so-called "is-ought problem."

6. Explain the difference between conceiving of happiness as a "terminus" and happiness as a "norm." What do you think of Aristotle's comment that we should call no man happy until he is dead?

7. Can we rightly call a person virtuous if he or she has acquired only some important virtues?

8. What are the central virtues in life?

9. Does being a good person guarantee one's happiness?

10. Is virtue its own reward?

11. Explain the way in which Jack and Steve relate the moral point of view to religion.

12. Is knowledge of ethics necessary for someone to be a good person?

Suggested Readings

Adler, Mortimer, *Aristotle for Everybody*, Macmillan, 1978. Part Two, "Man the Doer," supplies an excellent introduction to Aristotle's ethics. Our dialogue relies on Adler's discussion of the virtues and real versus apparent goods.

————, *Reforming Education*, Geraldine Van Doren, ed., Macmillan, 1988. This book contains several essays on moral philosophy written by Dr. Adler. The volume includes two book reviews that are especially noteworthy: "A Sound Moral Philosophy," a review of Alasdair MacIntyre's *After Virtue*, and "Ethics: Fourth Century B.C. and Twentieth Century A.D.," a review of Bernard Williams's *Ethics and the Limits of Philosophy*. These two reviews inspire some of the arguments presented in this dialogue.

————, *Six Great Ideas*, Macmillan, 1981. Especially good treatment of the "is-ought" problem. Our dialogue is clearly indebted to his argument here.

————, *Ten Philosophical Mistakes*, Collier Books, 1985. Contains another discussion of the is-ought problem and Aristotelian morality generally. Insightful discussion of the distinction between happiness as "norm" and "terminus."

Aquinas, St. Thomas, *Summa Theologiae*, Ottawa Institute of Medieval Studies, Ottawa, 1941. The second part elaborates on the virtues, moral and theological. Also contains a classic presentation of natural law morality.

Aristotle, *Nicomachean Ethics*, in *The Basic Works of Aristotle*, Richard McKeon, ed., Random House, 1941. The great Greek philosopher's definitive expression of virtue ethics.

MacIntyre, Alasdair, *After Virtue*, 2nd ed., University of Notre Dame Press, 1984. One of the most widely discussed books in ethics in the last decade. Offers a rich historical interpretation of moral philosophy leading to a new account of virtues. Peter's final cryptic comment about "Christianity or Nietzsche" relates to MacIntyre's work.

McInerny, Ralph, *Ethica Thomistica*, Catholic University of America Press, 1982. Highly readable summary of Aristotelian-Thomistic ethics. Helpful discussion of is-ought problem and of the virtues. Our dialogue relies on his interpretation of rationality and contemplation in Aristotle.

Nussbaum, Martha, *The Fragility of Goodness: Luck and Ethics in Greek Tragedy and Philosophy*, Cambridge University Press, 1986. Expresses a deep appreciation for the role of both virtue and good fortune for the good life.

Dialogue Eight:
Ethics and Female Voices

After the backpacking trip, Sophia meets her friend Anna at the Faculty Club on the campus of the university. Sophia is eager to discuss the work of Carol Gilligan, who holds that females typically approach moral situations in a distinctive manner. Peter and his friend Hobart join Sophia and Anna, and Hobart's contract view of morality is contrasted with what Gilligan calls the "care perspective." The dialogue ends with Peter tentatively suggesting that an ethic of care is important, but not a novel development in the history of moral thinking.

SOPHIA: Hi! I'm so glad you could meet me today. Pretty busy?

ANNA: As usual. Classes to prepare for, papers to grade, committee meetings, and not enough hours in the day.

SOPHIA: Well, I *had* to talk to you. I read Gilligan, as you suggested. After all those conversations on the backpacking trip that I told you about, I found it very interesting. Very interesting. I think I want to do something with my congregation on this material. Maybe a study group, maybe even a sermon.

ANNA: Good timing. We're doing Gilligan right now in my upper-level class. It always provokes a lot of discussion.

SOPHIA: Gilligan helped me to come to terms with my own experience. She . . . excuse me. Peter!

PETER: Sophia! How are you? I trust you've made the adjustment to civilization after our mountain experience.

SOPHIA: It was difficult. What a marvelous time we had. Won't you join us?

PETER: I'd be delighted. Let me introduce you to Hobart McKinney. He teaches in our Department of Political Science. Hobart, this is Sophia Woodward.

SOPHIA: And this is my friend, Anna Brandt, of the Women's Studies Department. Peter Simpson, Philosophy Department and mountain climber *extraordinaire*. Have you all met?

PETER: No. It's a big university. I'm pleased to meet you. I've heard excellent things about the Women's Studies Department.

SOPHIA: I feel like the odd person out among you academics. I scarcely have a paper to grade this week!

PETER: But a sermon to prepare? Or . . . do you call it a sermon? A lecture? A talk?

SOPHIA: No. A sermon, and it's one you should attend, *if* I do decide to write it. I saw Anna after I came back from the trip and I couldn't quit talking about our nightly "ethics" discussions. She suggested that I read Carol Gilligan's *In A Different Voice* for a feminist alternative to the kind of ideas we talked about. Have you read it, Peter? Hobart?

PETER: No, I haven't, but I know there's been considerable discussion of the book. One of my female colleagues in the philosophy department has mentioned it frequently. Hobart?

HOBART: No, I haven't read it. Mary Carlson in our department has accused me of being typically "male" in my political thinking, but I haven't taken the time to read Gilligan or any of the other feminists who have been doing work in political and moral theory. I wonder whether it's worth the effort. I'm not sure that feminism will be a sustainable intellectual project, at least in some of the more extreme forms it takes. It seems rather faddish. I'm more than eager to admit the historical inequities with regard to women, both political and moral inequities, and I've been active in the attempt to bolster the women's rights movement. But these more extreme positions . . . I wonder.

SOPHIA: What extreme positions?

HOBART: As I understand it, some feminists want to claim that much of the political and moral conceptual apparatus of Western civilization is somehow biased, somehow "male," whatever that means. As if our most deeply rooted philosophical concepts are skewed because most thinkers have been male. I have a difficult time accepting that, or even understanding what it might mean.

ANNA: I don't want to appear to be too unkind, Professor McKinney, but perhaps if you *read* some of the literature you might be able to grasp its significance.

HOBART: I'm perfectly open to persuasion. Can you help?

ANNA: I'm not prepared to speak for all feminists, and my own interests, as well as my academic background, are in psychology. As for the more radical critiques of the Western intellectual tradition, I'm not conversant enough with the literature to say much. I do find Gilligan's work on the psychology of moral development to be powerful and important.

PETER: But as I understand it, her work has had an influence on women *and* men interested in moral and political theory.

ANNA: Yes, it has.

SOPHIA: Professor McKinney . . .

HOBART: Please call me Hobart.

SOPHIA: Hobart, I'm interested in Gilligan because I want to make sense of my own moral experience, as a person, and as a *female*. I don't know whether Peter told you, but we recently met each other on a backpacking trip. Since Peter is a philosophy professor and he specializes in ethics, we asked him a few questions the first night and it led to a number of lengthy and interesting discussions about ethics. That's what I've been thinking about. I'm a Unitarian minister and I want to share these ideas and reflections with the people I minister to. I'm not interested in ivory-tower talk. I'm interested in real people, with real-life concerns, and I want them to have the opportunity to talk and think about the issues that we talked about in the mountains. I'm interested in what morality is about and how people think about what they should do in life. That's what we discussed, and in that context, as a real-life person, not an academic, I hear Gilligan saying something important, to *me*, to all of us.

PETER: Tell us what she says.

SOPHIA: I'll defer to Anna. But . . . I have an idea. In her research on moral development, Gilligan uses various examples and asks a series of questions of both women and men. She concludes that men and women hear different moral "voices," as she says. How about a miniexperiment here? I've talked to both Anna and Peter about these things, so let's have Hobart be our subject. Are you game?

HOBART: I suppose so.

SOPHIA: Tell us what you think morality is. Gilligan asks that and at some point describes various reactions. Just a moment. [She flips through the pages of *In A Different Voice*.] Here it is: "If you had to say what morality meant to you, how would you sum it up?" Well, Hobart? What would you say?

HOBART: Really, I'm no moral philosopher. I'm more interested in political theory.

SOPHIA: All the better. Maybe you'll be less abstract.

HOBART: I don't know about that, but I fear that my view of morality has been colored by my study of political philosophy.

SOPHIA: Indulge us.

HOBART: I hope my philosopher friend won't find this too naive, but to my mind, there's no great mystery about the source and purpose of what we call morality. Moral laws aren't written in some metaphysical heaven or grasped by some magical intuition of reason. Like most of the great thinkers in the Western tradition, I would attempt to understand morality by relating it to human nature—how we find ourselves and what kind of purposes we have. It's obvious that we have to live together and it also seems clear to me that even if we're not always ruthless egoists, we certainly tend to concern ourselves most with our own life, our own interests. In this sense, I believe that Hobbes was essentially correct to describe us as limited in our concern for others. Given this fact, it seems to me that morality is essentially a useful social device that is necessary if we want to have a civilized social life. Morality is constructed, or made. It's a useful, functional device to allow our situation to be enormously better than it might be without it. That's what I would say it is for.

PETER: If I may . . . Hobart, would you put this in contractual terms?

HOBART: Yes, I think so. Again, I don't find this particularly mysterious. I would admit that there was no explicit contract made, no point in history at which people *actually* got together and made the agreements that constitute the morality of a particular social or political group. But the idea of the contractual nature of morality is powerful as a kind of conceptual tool that shows *why* we have morality and *what* its central content is.

SOPHIA: And why do we have it?

HOBART: It's to each person's advantage to act according to certain central moral tenets, to teach these rules, to expect others to conform to them, generally, to reinforce the social institution as best we can. Our own lives benefit from this.

SOPHIA: What moral rules are you talking about?

HOBART: Obviously, to live together we have to have rules that prohibit unjustified killing or murder, theft, lying, and breaking promises. To have society, we can't have widespread violations of these norms. We reap the benefits of living in a social situation that prohibits such behavior, so there is a kind of implicit agreement involved. I agree to act in a certain way if you do. These basic rules apply to everyone equally, and when they are broken then various degrees of social censure are appropriate. If the rules are broken, then the underlying implicit social agreement is broken.

SOPHIA: Don't you think that morality consists of more than just telling the truth, not killing or stealing, and keeping your promises? Isn't there something deeper about morality?

HOBART: I would say that morality consists of a collection of rules or norms that rational, self-interested agents would agree to as the basis for social life. They are rules about what you can and cannot do in the pursuit of your own goals or purposes. Basically, as I see it, morality involves rules that tell us how to respect the rights of others, or not to violate the rights of others when we act. Peter, is this too naive for a philosopher to accept?

PETER: Not at all. It's a powerful perspective. It explains why we have morality, what its basic content is, what its status is, and why people ought to be moral.

SOPHIA: And why is that? Why should they be moral?

HOBART: Because it's in a person's interest to do so. If we respect the rights of each other, then each person can pursue his own individual vision of the good life as he sees fit, in an atmosphere of freedom and tolerance.

SOPHIA: So for you, society consists in a collection of independent, autonomous selves, who must choose for themselves how to live. And morality is the basis for an agreement that binds individuals together by the use of rules that apply fairly and equally to everyone. These rules are used to weigh competing interests, resolve conflicts, and help us choose a course of action that is right or fair. Is that it?

HOBART: Something like that.

SOPHIA: Well, Anna? You know Gilligan's work much better than I do, but that sounds exactly like the male approach to morality that she describes in her book.

HOBART: Male?

ANNA: She later calls it the *justice perspective* and she contrasts it with what she calls the *care perspective*, which she thinks is more typical of the way that females approach moral issues and frame moral alternatives. She believes that we tend to organize moral situations differently in terms of these two perspectives and that females typically think more in terms of care and responsibility than in terms of rights and rules and justice.

HOBART: What has this to do with being male or female?

SOPHIA: Anna, why don't you explain the main points in *In A Different Voice*?

PETER: Please do. I'd very much like to learn about Gilligan's work.

ANNA: You should keep in mind that Gilligan is primarily responding to certain theories of moral development, especially Kohlberg's, that have systematically ignored female experience.

PETER: So you take her to be responding primarily to psychologists?

ANNA: Yes, in the first instance, but her work has had a significant impact in other intellectual areas. Kohlberg's experiments used male subjects, and his theory of moral development stressed the notion that moral maturity involves the ability to reason abstractly, using and applying notions of human rights and justice. But females were found to be rather deficient in this type of abstract reasoning. Consequently, according to Kohlberg's theory, females would typically be judged as less developed, morally, than men.

SOPHIA: Morally immature?

ANNA: Yes. But Gilligan's research indicated that it was Kohlberg's scheme that was flawed, not women's ability to engage in moral thinking. She found that women think differently when they approach moral situations, not that they think badly or immaturely. And the distinctive way they think, the way they approach moral issues, the way they organize the elements of moral situations, is probably a function of the way they develop very early in life.

PETER: How so?

ANNA: According to some developmental theorists, the crucial psychological background is this: The personality structure of an individual is formed very early in life. In particular, gender identity, which is central to the formation of personality, is fixed by age three. But the process of forming an identity is quite different in males and females. Since the mother is the primary caretaker, the relationships of children to their mothers are fundamental. Little girls experience themselves as female, like their mothers, and their identity develops in the context of feelings of attachment and connectedness. Little boys develop an identity that stresses the centrality of individuation, they experience themselves as separate from their mothers, and the notion of a masculine identity emphasizes this separateness and independence.

SOPHIA: So feelings of connection or attachment to others, to the world, are typical of the development of females.

ANNA: Yes. Females tend to develop with stronger feelings of connectedness to other people, and this is important for the way they approach moral situations.

PETER: I see. According to psychologists, feminine identity is closely associated with being related, or connected, to others, as you say, whereas masculine identity develops with a stronger emphasis on being separate, or individuated. I think I can see where this is going in relation to moral theory. But please go on.

HOBART: I'm already suspicious of these psychological explanations of how everything is really determined by age three, or four, or six, or whatever they happen to be saying now. Obviously, one of the things we do with all children, if we want to educate them morally, is to help them to feel some sympathy or attachment to others. But we also want the child to be an individual, whether male or female, to be able to make his or her own choices, and to be able to take control of his or her own life, at least at some point.

SOPHIA: Whatever the explanation, if the research shows that there actually *are* the kind of gender differences that Gilligan talks about, you can't discount it.

HOBART: I'm not discounting anything. I'm merely saying that, wherever we're going with this psychological theorizing, it already seems to me that it's a mistake to talk about little *boys* being individuals and little *girls* being attached to others. Why not say that, as people, as parents, we face the task of developing as individuals *and* as members of groups and teaching our children appropriately?

ANNA: I think Gilligan agrees with that, but, as a matter of fact, theories of moral development have stressed a view of moral maturity that emphasizes a particular view of the self and its relation to others. And that view is, in fact, one-sided. Plus, Sophia is right. The issue is, in part, empirical. Gilligan's studies have shown that there *are* gender differences in the way females and males approach moral issues, and real differences will have real effects in the real world when people think about real issues.

HOBART: It's still not clear to me what these supposed differences are.

SOPHIA: May I?

ANNA: Go ahead.

SOPHIA: Early in the book, Gilligan discusses an example that Kohlberg used. In the example, a man, Heinz, needs a drug to save his wife's life. He doesn't have enough money to buy it, and evidently the druggist won't sell it for less, so the man must decide whether to steal the drug to save the life of his wife. Eleven-year-old boys and girls were asked whether the man should steal the drug and then were asked follow-up questions. Gilligan focuses on the answers of one boy and one girl as typical.

HOBART: Rather small example.

SOPHIA: There were numerous examples in the book. Anyway, the little boy, Jake, used logic in a precise way. He applied rules perfectly, weighed the value of life higher than the value of property, and had no problem resolving the conflict. Steal the drug. But the little girl, Amy, had a much more difficult time. She didn't see the situation as simply applying abstract rules with logical precision, she saw much more complexity in the situation. She seemed more uncertain. She realized that if the man stole the drug, other things would happen. He might go to jail, which would have a terrible impact on the wife. She might get worse. She didn't think the wife should die, but she didn't think the man should steal. She wanted to consider other options. She wanted the man to talk it out with the druggist, to get them together, to communicate to resolve the issue. She saw a whole web of complex relationships in which the people were connected because courses of action could hurt one another and real consequences had to be considered.

ANNA: For Gilligan, what would appear to some psychologists as hedging and moral immaturity is really a different approach. The little boy sees the situation as involving the application of rules and a strict hierarchy of values, to be unambiguously resolved by logic or abstract reason. She also talks about the differences between the play of girls and boys. Boys tend to play games with rules that apply fairly to everyone to resolve disputes. Girls, in their play, tend to be concerned with relationships. In the druggist example, the little girl is much more attentive to the particular details of the situation. She is sensitive to the need for a contextual judgment that doesn't gloss over the relationships involved. She sees the need for care on the part of the druggist, for *response*.

SOPHIA: Here's what Gilligan says on page twenty-nine: "Instead, seeing a world comprised of relationships rather than of people standing alone, a world that coheres through human connection rather than through systems of rules, she finds the puzzle in the dilemma to lie in the failure of the druggist to respond to the wife."

ANNA: Read the passage further on down the page. Here.

SOPHIA: "Both children thus recognize the need for agreement but see it as mediated in different ways—he impersonally through systems of logic and law, she personally through communication in relationships."

ANNA: It also seems to me that the little girl approached the situation with more feeling than just abstractly and impersonally applying rules.

PETER: But there is certainly a kind of logic in her response. You say it's a contextual thinking, and it is guided by the notions of care and attachment.

ANNA: I think it's a different kind of logic.

PETER: So for you, or for Gilligan, a morality that centers on rights and rules stresses a view of the individual as essentially separate or isolated. In this sense, Hobart's contractual view fits into this category. Morality requires the use of rules that are impartially applied by rational, self-interested individuals to resolve conflicts fairly, to make social life possible, to make *individual,* autonomous life possible.

ANNA: Yes, whereas a female typically approaches moral situations with an eye toward what she calls "activities of care" that reinforce the bonds of relationships that *connect* us, that make us feel responsible for others in a deeper and sensitive way. That's *not* moral immaturity. The care perspective calls for responsiveness and real sensitivity. But it makes moral reasoning more than just logic chopping or abstract application of rules.

SOPHIA: I was especially struck by the difference between seeing moral problems abstractly and seeing the actual stories of peoples' lives involved in difficult choices.

ANNA: Gilligan at one point contrasts seeing a moral problem as a kind of math problem, like the little boy, and reconstructing, either in our moral imagination or our immediate apprehension of real situations, a narrative of the connections and relationships that develop. It's as if one approach to moral reasoning just focuses on the moment as an isolated instant in time, to be coldly analyzed by using your rational scales to "weigh" the values involved. The other sees the moment as part of a process, as a moment in the history of people with stories that involve complex relationships, the need for response, and caring activities that reinforce connection.

SOPHIA: That comes out best in Gilligan's abortion study. I wish every male prolifer would read that chapter. It's really very striking. The whole abortion debate is a great example of the conflict in these two moral perspectives. All you hear about is weighing "rights," as if one case is the same as the next. But these situations are very specific, very particular. Context is so important when a woman has to decide what to do in this situation. And it's precisely because of the importance of context that absolute laws dictating personal choice are so unrealistic. Women see the abortion issue not just in terms of the so-called "rights" of the fetus, but in terms of her relationships, the web of connections within which the pregnancy occurred. Some prolifers talk as if all women in this situation are just "irresponsible." But it's because a woman is so sensitive to an ethic of responsibility to her lover, to her family, to the developing fetus, and even to herself, that the decision is so excruciatingly difficult.

ANNA: Gilligan sums this up nicely on page one hundred. "The moral imperative that emerges repeatedly in interviews with women is an injunction to care, a responsibility to discern and alleviate the real and recognizable trouble of this world. For men, the moral imperative appears rather as an injunction to respect the rights of others and thus to protect from interference the rights to life and self-fulfillment. . . . For men, recognition through experience of the need for more active responsibility in taking care corrects the potential indifference of a morality of noninterference and turns attention from the logic to the consequences of choice."

HOBART: But I don't understand this. You say that the emphasis on a morality of rights is somehow more "male," at least in the assumption of individuals as more separate from the community, as autonomous agents. But what about all the talk about women's *rights*, about the right to choose, the right to pursue a career of choice, the right to equitable pay? How can you claim all these rights for women, yet at the same time criticize a morality of rights as an expression of gender bias?

ANNA: I think Gilligan recognizes this tension. She has a chapter on women's rights. Here, page 132: "But a further problem arises from the tension between a morality of rights that dissolves 'natural bonds' in support of individual claims and a morality of responsibility that knits such claims into a fabric of relationship, blurring the distinction between self and other through the representation of their interdependence."

HOBART: So how is this so-called "tension" resolved? Is it a tension, or an outright inconsistency?

ANNA: It's a tension, and one that is not easily resolved or explained away. It's lived, in our experiences of trying to work out the conflict between our own legitimate interests as individuals and the responsibilities we feel because of interdependence with others.

SOPHIA: It means for us that these moral ideals must complement each other. They're not really separate or contradictory. The women's rights movement has been crucial for women to think more of their own needs and not to accept the feminine ideal as one of absolute self-denial or submergence into a family context.

ANNA: That's precisely what she says. In talking about the women's movement of the 1970s, here's what she says on page 149 about female college students: "Questioning the stoicism of self-denial and replacing the illusion of innocence with an awareness of choice, they struggled to grasp the essential notion of rights, that the interests of the self can be considered legitimate. In this sense, the concept of rights changes women's conceptions of self, allowing them to see themselves as stronger and to consider directly their own needs. When assertion no longer seems dangerous, the concept of relationships changes from a bond of continuing dependence to a dynamic of interdependence. Then the notion of care expands from the paralyzing injunction not to hurt others to an injunction to act responsively toward self and others and thus to sustain connection." She says women can now season mercy with justice and care for themselves as well as others.

HOBART: I agree. I totally agree. But you talk as if Gilligan's work is important because she calls attention to the *distinctive* moral voice of women. Now you say that the two perspectives are complementary. How distinctive can a women's morality of care be if it must be mediated by the morality of justice or rights that is criticized as being a product of male bias or a product of a masculine emphasis on detachment and individuation?

ANNA: It's certainly distinctive in the sense that it is a legitimate way to approach moral situations and make difficult particular choices, it appears to be more typical of the moral development of females, and when females score at a morally immature level on Kohlberg's scale this distinctiveness is ignored and even ridiculed.

HOBART: So once again you see Gilligan's position primarily in the context of psychological theory that uncritically accepts a certain view of morality as *the* exclusive moral perspective.

ANNA: Yes, but this whole emphasis on rights and separate individuals obviously has effects on our society, on the moral and political discourse that are prevalent. If we emphasize the bonds of connection that knit together the life of a community rather than an abstract contractual agreement that contingently relates us to one another, then our social life and our social judgments will change. It will affect how we think of our social institutions and our community problems. We should care about the homeless, we should care about the image of women in advertising and pornography, we should care about ruthless plant closings in communities and about the effects of environmental hazards on people. If we see how connections to smaller groups, to communities that are deeply a part of our *individual* stories, are central to what we are, it will change how we judge the public activities of government and how we live our life. What has happened to our public life, our feelings of community? I believe all of these issues are related to the feminist emphasis on connection and care and responsibility.

SOPHIA: Peter, you haven't said much for awhile. As a philosopher, what do you think about Gilligan's ideas?

PETER: I'm somewhat hesitant to say anything, since I haven't studied Gilligan's work. This is extremely interesting, but I'm not sure that it's so very novel, at least from the standpoint of moral philosophy.

SOPHIA: You don't think her ideas are important?

PETER: No, that's certainly not what I said. It seems to me that the emphasis on care in morality is very important, but there's nothing terribly new about this perspective. For example, as I understand how you have described Gilligan's analysis of typically female moral thinking, it tends to be contextual, highly particularistic. The little girl in the original example wanted to fill in, or at least imagine, a lot of particular details that would be important. Is that right?

ANNA: Yes. Just a moment. . . . Here's another passage starting on page one hundred: "The proclivity of women to reconstruct hypothetical dilemmas in terms of the real, to request or to supply missing information about the nature of the people and the places where they live, shifts their judgment away from the hierarchical ordering of principles and the formal procedures of decision making. This insistence on the particular signifies an orientation to the dilemma and to moral problems in general that differs from any current developmental stage description."

PETER: Of course, I can't speak about psychological theories of development, but the emphasis on context, on the *particular* nature of moral situations, has long been emphasized in the history of moral philosophy. Aristotle emphasizes that a judgment of practical reason, for example, when we have to decide whether to be truthful or totally honest, is highly contextual. Honesty is a virtue, and in some situations it's not only possible to be dishonest, one can also be *too* honest, when one might hurt someone's feelings by being "brutally" honest, as they say. There's no precise mathematical formula, no algorithm to show how one ought to act. It depends on the situation and personal experience. Likewise, if you take care to be your central moral virtue, then being a caring person will be a product of making caring choices in a variety of particular situations. And how that is done, how one becomes a caring person, is highly contextual. I see Gilligan's emphasis on care and context as fitting quite nicely into the tradition of virtue ethics. Also, any ethical theory that emphasizes the application of a very general principle to every specific situation would have to emphasize the particularities of context.

SOPHIA: Like consequentialism?

PETER: Yes. Act utilitarianism emphasizes the particularities of situations in just this way.

SOPHIA: That's interesting. Anna, hand me Gilligan's book. . . . I thought about this because of our discussions on the backpacking trip. There are times when women talk about morality in ways that are strikingly similar to consequentialism or utilitarianism. I made a note of these. On page twenty-one, a women says she values "having other people that I'm tied to, and also having people that I am responsible to. I have a very strong sense of being responsible to the world, that I can't just live for my enjoyment, but just the fact of being in the world gives me an obligation to do what I can to make the world a better place to live in, no matter how small a scale that may be." Then Gilligan says, "Thus while Kohlberg's subject worries about people interfering with each other's rights, this woman worries about 'the possibility of omission, of your not helping others when you could help them.' " We talked about this on the trip. That sounds very much like a consequentialist moral approach that expects us to promote as much good as possible. Remember, we talked about how demanding this view is. That's what this woman is saying.

PETER: And recall that you questioned a morality of respect for persons precisely on these grounds, that it might lead to a kind of moral minimalism in which the primary injunction is not to harm others rather than actively feeling an obligation to help them.

SOPHIA: Or care for them.

PETER: Yes.

SOPHIA: Listen to this passage on page fifty-four. Gilligan is talking about a mature woman who responds to the druggist example. "Just as Claire considers the druggist morally responsible for his refusal, so she ties morality to an awareness of connection, defining the moral person as one who, in acting, 'seriously considers the consequences to everybody involved.' " That sounds just like utilitarianism.

ANNA: But utilitarianism is calculative, isn't it? Don't you just mathematically count up pleasures and pains to see which action has the best results? That's not the way that Gilligan describes the injunction to care. It's not mathematical at all. It's more a matter of feeling and moral imagination.

PETER: I often think the utilitarian emphasis on calculation is misleading, more a metaphor for the attention to consequences than an accurate description of how we actually think when we consider the effects of our actions on others. We can't actually *quantify* such things as human happiness. In any case, we might just describe the ethic of care as a kind of noncalculative consequentialism, if its primary norm is to care for others. In this sense, it appears to be an expression of what many moral philosophers have emphasized using other terms, like benevolence or charity or even love. I also think that one could express this ethic in either the language of virtue or the language of an ethic of duty or principle. But as we've already said, and as *many* moral thinkers have also suggested, there may be at least two fundamental perspectives in morality. Gilligan and other feminists aren't offering us anything new or novel. Perhaps they're right to point out that the language of rights, so prevalent in our public moral and political discourse, tends to mask, either explicitly or implicitly, a *kind* of moral indifference, or a possible attitude of indifference, toward the suffering that we might alleviate.

ANNA: She has a wonderful way of putting this in another piece. She says we're all vulnerable both to "oppression and abandonment." If the language of justice and rights is crucial for responding to oppression, then the language of care is important for capturing our need to respond to feelings of abandonment in people. That's why a morality emphasizing connectedness is important.

SOPHIA: We do have these feelings of connection with others. That's why I've decided that an ethic of pure egoism or self-interest is misguided. If what we are depends on our relationships, our connections, the way we live our stories together, then there's no sharp distinction between acting for one's *self-interest* and acting exclusively for *others*. My self involves others.

PETER: I'm sorry, but I must go. Students await me. Hobart?

HOBART: I should go also. Professor Brandt, Ms. Woodward, you've given me much to think about. I shall take your remarks as a challenge and see what these feminists are talking about. Thanks so much for an interesting discussion.

What Thinkers Have Said

In describing an alternative standpoint, I will reconstruct the account of moral development around two moral perspectives, grounded in different dimensions of relationship that give rise to moral concern. The justice perspective, often equated with moral reasoning, is recast as one way of seeing moral problems and a care perspective is brought forward as an alternate vision or frame. The distinction between justice and care as alternative perspectives or moral orientations is based empirically on the observation that a shift in the focus of attention from concerns about justice to concerns about care changes the definition of what constitutes a moral problem, and leads the same situation to be seen in different ways. Theoretically, the distinction between justice and care cuts across the familiar divisions between thinking and feeling, egoism and altruism, theoretical and practical reasoning. It calls attention to the fact that all human relationships public and private, can be characterized both in terms of equality and in terms of attachment, and that both inequality and detachment constitute grounds for moral concern. Since everyone is vulnerable both to oppression and to abandonment, two moral visions —one of justice and one of care—recur in human experience. The moral injunctions, not to act unfairly toward others, and not to turn away from someone in need, capture these different concerns.

Carol Gilligan, "Moral Orientation and Moral Development"

From a justice perspective, the self as moral agent stands as the figure against a ground of social relationships, judging the conflicting claims of self and others against a standard of equality or equal respect (the Categorical Imperative, the Golden Rule). From a care perspective, the relationship becomes the figure, defining self and others. Within the context of relationship, the self as a moral agent perceives and responds to the perception of need. The shift in moral perspective is manifest by a change in the moral question from "What is just?" to "How to respond?"

Carol Gilligan, "Moral Orientation and Moral Development"

As a moral perspective, care is less well elaborated, and there is no ready vocabulary in moral theory to describe its terms. As a framework for moral decision, care is grounded in the assumption that self and other are interdependent, an assumption reflected in a view of action as responsive and, therefore, as arising in relationship rather than the view of action as emanating from within the self and, therefore, "self-governed." Seen as responsive, the self is by definition connected to others, responding to perceptions, interpreting events, and governed by the organizing tendencies of human interaction and human language. Within this framework, detachment, whether from self or from others, is morally problematic, since it breeds moral blindness or indifference—a failure to discern or respond to need. The question of what responses constitute care and what responses lead to hurt draws attention to the fact that one's own terms may differ from those of others. Justice in this context becomes understood as respect for people in their own terms.

Carol Gilligan, "Moral Orientation and Moral Development"

... [W]e believe that Gilligan's distinction between a morality of care and a morality of justice is a distinction held in the minds of all human beings, be they male or female. . . . In our view, however, these two senses of the word moral do not represent two different moral orientations existing at the same level of generality and validity. We see justice as both rational and implying an attitude of empathy. It is for this reason that we make the following proposal: that is, that there is a dimension along which various moral dilemmas and orientations can be placed. Personal moral dilemmas and orientations of special obligation . . . represent one end of this dimension, and the standard hypothetical justice dilemmas and justice orientations represent the other end.

Lawrence Kohlberg, *The Psychology of Moral Development*

Key Terms and Concepts

contract theory of morality

justice perspective

moral maturity

activities of care

connection vs. individual rights

care as a virtue

contextualism

oppression and abandonment

Questions

1. Does Gilligan's emphasis on gender differences in moral thinking coincide with your own approach to moral situations? That is, if you are female, do you typically tend to construct moral situations as Gilligan describes? What is your reaction to Gilligan's views?

2. Do you believe that boys and girls are still socialized quite differently in our society? Do you believe this justifies the claim that there are gender differences in moral decision making?

3. What are the strengths and weaknesses of Hobart's contractual view of morality?

4. What is moral "maturity"? Put negatively, what are symptoms of immaturity in moral decision making?

5. Summarize Peter's critical response to Gilligan's views about female moral voices. Do you agree?

6. Would an ethics of "care" or connectedness lead toward a prochoice or prolife position on abortion? Explain your answer.

7. After reading these dialogues, would you say that Gilligan has accurately described the kind of moral reasoning that she characterizes as typically "male"? Is it misleading to accept Kohlberg's description of mature moral reasoning as representative of a "male" tradition in ethics?

Suggested Readings

Gilligan, Carol, *In A Different Voice: Psychological Theory and Women's Development*, Harvard University Press, 1982.

Gilligan, Carol, "Moral Orientation and Moral Development," in *Women and Moral Theory*, Eva Kittay and Diana T. Myers, eds., Rowman and Littlefield, 1987. This is an important article summarizing her position, explaining it more concisely, and updating her research. The book as a whole is an informative collection.

Kohlberg, Lawrence, *The Psychology of Moral Development*, Vol II, Harper and Row, 1984. In this volume, Kohlberg replies to Gilligan.

Epilogue:
Is Ethics Worthwhile?

*Two weeks after coming back from the backpacking trip, most of the partici-
pants have gathered for a party at Peter's house. Sarah and Ransom suggested that
it would be an enjoyable way to conclude their experience together. They have
eaten supper, the evening is getting late, and their reunion is drawing to a close.
Let's listen to the final part of their conversation.*

ALICE: I've found it so hard to get back in the rhythm of things.

SOPHIA: So true. I keep thinking about those glorious sunny days
at eight thousand feet and those wonderful crisp evenings with the
breeze blowing through the pines. No noises. No TV. No civilization!

MARK: I can see why a fellow like Donovan might want to live
up there. But you have to make a living. I don't know what I'd do
for work in the mountains.

PETER: Speaking of Donovan, I saw him yesterday at the library.
I told him about our party tonight. I hoped he would come, but
with Donovan you never know. He's very unpredictable.

BOB: What was he doing in town?

PETER: He has relatives that live here. He also comes back from
time to time to buy books.

BOB: So, Peter, are you ready for the fall term?

PETER: Almost. My preparation is complete and I have one more
syllabus to type.

SARAH: Teaching ethics again?

PETER: Oh, yes. And I have some new ideas to work on because
of our discussions on the trip.

At this point someone knocks on the door. Peter crosses the room, opens the door, and greets Donovan.

PETER: Donovan! We'd just about given up on you. Please come in.

DONOVAN: Not bad, Peter. Not bad at all. Poor Socrates. He didn't have much, but you tenured professional philosophers must not do too badly. Nice place.

PETER: You remember all of these people?

DONOVAN: Of course! When we finally talked like real people that last night at Lost Lake, we got to know each other. Hello, Sophia. Bob, Mark, Alice, Sarah, Ransom. See? You would have had a great time if you'd have left your philosopher friend home and not wasted those nights flapping your jaws about philosophy. Eh, Professor?

PETER: [Smiling.] Always the irrepressible gadfly, Donovan! You'll not provoke me tonight.

DONOVAN: Please, give me some time. The night is young. Don't let me interrupt your conversation. Just get me a beer! Carry on.

SOPHIA: I'm afraid you came in just at the moment that Peter was telling us about the ethics course he will teach this fall. Evidently, we had some effect on what he'll talk about.

DONOVAN: Ethics courses! Bah! Humbug! A complete waste of time.

SARAH: Get to the point, Donovan. Don't mince words!

DONOVAN: Have I provoked you yet, my old friend?

PETER: Not one whit!

BOB: Well, you've provoked me. I've taken some summer courses in which we discussed philosophical ethics. And our conversations in the mountains were somewhat like nightly classes. Tell us why you think ethics courses are a "waste of time," as you say.

DONOVAN: It's a cottage industry. It's boom time for ethics professors. People moan about the moral decline of the West, about the moral vacuum in our society. So there's a scramble to provide ethics instruction. Ethics. Business ethics. Medical ethics. Engineering ethics. Ad nauseam. A complete waste of time. You don't make people better by giving them courses in ethics. By the time people take these courses, they either have good character or they don't. It's a matter of training, not thinking. It's a matter of having good parents; it doesn't depend on being a good philosopher or asking questions like "What would a utilitarian say about that?" You don't make people better by having them take useless ethics courses.

PETER: That's simply not the main purpose of ethics. It may be a side effect or a corollary, but that's certainly not my goal when I teach ethics or engage in ethical reflection.

SOPHIA: Then what is the purpose, Peter?

PETER: I don't think there is any *one* purpose. I think a number of things can and do happen when a person takes an ethics course or converses about ethical matters, as we did.

SOPHIA: Such as?

PETER: First of all, I think ethical reflection provides an opportunity for self-reflection. I don't know how many times I've heard one of my students say things like, "I didn't realize I was so . . ." and then explains the way in which our discussions in class helped him clarify or even discover what kind of moral beliefs he held, at least implicitly. I believe ethical reflection can aid the development of *self-knowledge*.

SARAH: Do you mean asking yourself whether you're really, basically, an egoist, or a utilitarian?

BOB: Or a Kantian? Or believe natural law provides the answer?

MARK: Don't forget Ransom's Divine Command ethics.

PETER: That's certainly part of it. We can ask ourselves what we believe and why we believe the way we do. We may, for the first time, realize what our basic principles are. And we may also think about issues we've never thought about before.

DONOVAN: Wonderful. Ethics as "values clarification." Just what we need. More of the kind of nonsense we've gotten from the social sciences for years. Let's all hold hands and tell each other what we really feel. How boring! I remember teaching the obligatory discussion section of "Moral Problems" in graduate school. The students were so wonderfully predictable. They said the same things, over and over. Perfect expressions of their culture, their parents, their religion. What good is self-knowledge when it's knowledge of the trivial and banal?

PETER: I always felt you consistently underestimated students, at least *some* students. I agree with part of what you say. Some are rather tame and unreflective products of their upbringing. But ethics isn't simply a matter of clarifying what we actually believe. It also must involve *self-criticism*. Yes, we are all products. But as reflective creatures we have the ability to ask whether our conventional moral beliefs can be rationally justified. There is an important distinction sometimes offered by moral philosophers. They distinguish *customary* and *reflective* morality. A person can simply take over what's she's been taught by her parents or her culture. But she can also subject customary or conventional morality to philosophical criticism. There is an important sense in which ethics can, in fact, make us better people. If it is better to be autonomous, that is, to decide for ourselves how to live, and ethical reflection is an important element in the development of autonomy, then I think taking an ethics course can, in fact, make a person better.

DONOVAN: Oh, come on, Peter. Are you still trying to save the world? You go into the classroom, trot out your arguments, and your students leave unchanged. You give them your knockdown arguments for vegetarianism—I've seen you in action—and they leave, very impressed. They even continue to discuss the ideas as they chomp into a juicy hamburger at the local campus grill.

PETER: Sometimes, but not always. Some students *are* changed by reflection. But even if they are not, there may be an honest difference of opinion about what the best arguments are. Subjecting the beliefs of conventional morality to criticism doesn't mean you must reject them. You may reflect on what you have been taught and find that your moral beliefs can stand the test of criticism.

DONOVAN: Or you may use the sophisticated arguments you learn in ethics to enable you to rationalize whatever you do, in fact, decide to do—or not to do.

PETER: Again, I understand the strength of the cultural forces and the personal family forces at work when a person acts, or expresses his beliefs, or is confronted by challenging opposing arguments. Character is, in part, shaped early. But virtue can be reshaped by the choices we make, by the reflection we engage in. I just don't believe we are molded for life by the time we reach the age of reflection. Rational criticism in ethics can be effective.

SOPHIA: How?

PETER: Look at the way our discussions progressed. We are already involved in the moral life when we begin to engage in philosophical, that is, ethical, reflection. For example, we can always ask whether the system of moral beliefs we already have is *consistent*. When we make quite general claims about moral rightness or morality we can attempt to investigate the *consequences* of holding such views. Recall the way we criticized the Divine Command Theory, and normative relativism, and utilitarianism.

BOB: There's no doubt in my own mind that we were able to show that some of these doctrines are simply not acceptable as theories of our moral life.

PETER: Many philosophers would agree with your point. At the least, in ethics we can narrow the range of rationally plausible candidates for an acceptable ethical theory.

SOPHIA: Let me say that the one thing I took away from our discussions is the recognition of the difficulty of these questions. These are very complex issues, easily oversimplified. I'm struck by this fact when I go into a mall bookstore now and see titles like

Looking Out for Number One or I see one of Ayn Rand's titles on the shelf. I think we want things to be simple, in morality as elsewhere, and there's always someone available to convince unthinking people that there are "black-and-white" answers.

BOB: I'm also impressed by the way in which ethics can make us more sensitive to the dimensions of the moral sphere. Sometimes good people don't realize that the things they do, like littering for example, may have some moral significance.

PETER: Nicely said. I like the notion of ethics as a "sensitizing" activity. It's very striking when you're around people who have studied moral philosophy. It's as if we can become more open to moral arguments, or at least we can get into the habit of considering actions from the moral point of view. But there is one more important goal of ethics. Some philosophers would say that we have ignored the primary purpose of ethics.

SOPHIA: Which is?

PETER: Theoretical, not practical. After all, ethics, as a discipline, is a part of philosophy. Philosophy seeks knowledge. It might be a mistake to think that the justification of ethics must be based solely on its practical significance. As a speculative activity, it seeks a theoretical understanding of the first principles of our moral life. A philosopher might be a very bad person, but it is still worthwhile in itself to seek to understand morality. Such conceptual clarity, if it could be achieved, would be valuable in its own right. In the end, perhaps ethics is about knowledge. Secondarily, if you have knowledge, it might affect your life.

DONOVAN: Hopeless. You're hopeless. Ethics is hopeless. Philosophy is hopeless. You seek what can't be found.

PETER: So you engage us in philosophical debate to show us that philosophy is hopeless? Are you being consistent, Donovan?

DONOVAN: Touché! Perhaps I should be more careful. Philosophy, as you practice it in ethics, is hopeless. Better?

PETER: Somewhat, although I still deeply disagree with you.

DONOVAN: Don't you want *the* correct theory? Aren't you looking for *the* correct theoretical picture of our moral life? You see, Sophia was right on track. These empty-headed popular moralizers do oversimplify. But so does traditional moral philosophy. Even if I agree that philosophical ethics can "narrow the range of plausible candidates," you still have the problem of choosing between or among theories that appear to be internally consistent and intuitively attractive. How does one do that, rationally? Eh, Peter? And each theory doesn't quite get it. Each reduces the complexity of life to a more simple, and therefore false theoretical structure. Give it up! Give up the attempt to find a tidy theory.

PETER: I think you overestimate what we should expect from an ethical theory. We shouldn't give up all of the positive aspects of ethical reflection, the very ones we have just talked about, just because there may be some doubt about whether we can tie up all the loose ends. And some philosophers simply disagree with you. Ethical theory can succeed.

DONOVAN: Then there's the problem of why we should accept the values of morality as the most important ones in our life.

PETER: If you're now asking, "Why be moral?," I'd be willing to take up that question, but I fear our friends are growing weary of these discussions.

SOPHIA: I'm getting tired, but not because of these discussions. Maybe we could get together next week.

DONOVAN: And someday you'll return to the mountains and tell me all about it. Good night, all!

What Thinkers Have Said

There is certainly a place for philosophical reflection on the existence and nature of values. But its practical significance is nil. Telling right from wrong in everyday life is not that hard; the hard part is overcoming laziness and cowardice to do what one perfectly well knows one should. As every parent learns, only good examples and apt incentives can induce that strength.

Michael Levin, "Ethics Courses: Useless"

Since moral philosophy systematically explores questions of human conduct, one studies the writings of moral philosophers in order to clarify one's own thinking on these questions. The writings of moral philosophers can illuminate facets of our experience, revealing a significance we had not fully appreciated. They can bring to our attention and force us to examine critically things we had taken for granted. They may show us that our beliefs have implications or interconnections we were not aware of and perhaps even that among our beliefs are inconsistencies we had not noticed, and they can suggest new lines of thought for us to pursue.

Jack Glickman, *Moral Philosophy: An Introduction*

If it is better for us to avoid holding inconsistent moral principles and to understand the principles we hold; and if it is better for us to be clear about the consequences of our moral principles and to be skeptical about faddish moral doctrines, then the careful study of moral philosophy can help us to be better persons.

Fred Feldman, *Introductory Ethics*

Moral growth occurs, then, as the individual develops the capacity to reason about his moral beliefs. Instead of blindly adopting his society's moral code or being easily shocked by the moral systems of other cultures, he is able to think clearly, calmly, and coherently about any set of moral norms. He learns how to give good reasons for accepting and rejecting such norms, or else he learns the limits of moral reasoning, or why no such reasoning is possible. But whatever might be his conclusions, they are arrived at on the basis of his own reflection. He can then decide for himself what standards of evaluation and rules of conduct to commit himself to.

Paul Taylor, *Principles of Ethics*

Moral philosophy is one area of philosophy in which the "linguistic turn," as it has been called, has not helped to give problems a more tractable shape. This is not to deny that moral philosophy, like other parts of philosophy, is properly concerned with reflection on what we say. Indeed, at one level it might have done better than it has if it had been more concerned with what we say. Its prevailing fault, in all its styles, is to impose on ethical life some immensely simple model, whether it be of the concepts that we actually use or of moral rules by which we should be guided. One remedy to this persistent deformation might indeed have been to attend to the great diversity of things that people do say about how they and other people live their lives.

Bernard Williams, *Ethics and the Limits of Philosophy*

We must be content, then, in speaking of such subjects and with such premises to indicate the truth roughly and in outline, and in speaking about things which are only for the most part true and with premises of the same kind to reach conclusions that are no better. In the same spirit, therefore, should each type of statement be received; for it is the mark of an educated man to look for precision in each class of things just so far as the nature of the subject admits; it is evidently equally foolish to accept probable reasoning from a mathematician and to demand from a rhetorician scientific proofs.

Aristotle, *Nichomachean Ethics*

Suggested Readings

Feldman, Fred, *Introductory Ethics,* Prentice-Hall, 1978. Contains a brief and insightful discussion of the value of moral philosophy.

Glickman, Jack, ed., *Moral Philosophy: An Introduction,* St. Martin's Press, 1976. The "Introduction" is the source of one of the quotations.

Levin, Michael, "Ethics Courses: Useless," *New York Times,* November 25, 1989. A pointed condemnation of ethics education in universities.

Taylor, Paul, *Principles of Ethics,* Dickenson, 1975. Explains the difference between "customary morality" and "reflective morality" and defends the value of ethics.

Williams, Bernard, *Ethics and the Limits of Philosophy,* Harvard University Press, 1985. Sophisticated but readable criticism of the traditional project of moral theory.